ANTIGUA AND BARBUDA TRAVEL GUIDE

Discover the Must-See Attractions, Things to Do, Hotels, Itinerary, Beaches, Culture and Food of the Caribbean's Gem

CLARA CARTER

TABLE OF CONTENTS

INTRODUCTION

Hello, fellow travel enthusiast! As you flip through the pages of this travel guide, allow me to whisk you away to the sun-kissed haven of Antigua and Barbuda through the lens of my own unforgettable adventure.

Picture this: A warm breeze carrying the scent of saltwater and the rhythmic sound of waves gently lapping against the shore. That's the embrace of Antigua, welcoming you with open arms. As I stepped onto the powdery white sands of Jumby Bay Island, the cares of the world melted away. This private retreat, nestled amidst turquoise waters, became my sanctuary.

My journey led me to the historic Nelson's Dockyard, where time seemed to stand still. Amidst cobblestone streets and restored colonial buildings, I delved into the maritime history of Antigua. The tales whispered by the sea breeze painted vivid pictures of a bygone era, leaving me in awe of the island's rich heritage.

A highlight etched in my memory was the enchanting Stingray City. Snorkeling with these graceful creatures in the crystal-clear waters was nothing short of magical. It felt like entering an underwater realm, where these gentle rays danced around, creating a surreal ballet beneath the Caribbean sun.

Barbuda, with its untouched beauty, offered a serene contrast. The pink sand beaches beckoned, and I found myself lost in the tranquility of Barbuda Belle. This boutique escape on the northwestern coast was a cocoon of luxury, with the ocean as my backdrop and the soft rustle of palm trees as my soundtrack.

Exploring the Frigate Bird Sanctuary in Codrington Lagoon was a nature lover's dream. Witnessing the majesty of these birds, soaring against the backdrop of the blue sky, was a moment of pure serenity. Barbuda, with its simplicity and untouched landscapes, spoke to my soul in a way I never expected.

As the sun dipped below the horizon, Shirley Heights Lookout became my haven for Sunday barbecues and panoramic views. The reggae tunes mingling with the aroma of jerk chicken created an atmosphere that encapsulated the essence of Caribbean bliss.

My journey was more than a series of destinations; it was a tapestry woven with the vibrant threads of Antiguan and Barbudan culture. From the lively markets bursting with color to the rhythmic beats of local music, every moment felt like a celebration of life.

And now, my fellow explorer, as you embark on your own adventure through the pages of this guide, I extend an invitation. Let the stories shared here be the compass guiding you to your own memorable experiences in Antigua and Barbuda. May your journey be filled with the warmth of the sun, the embrace of the sea, and the echoes of laughter that linger in these tropical paradises. Safe travels!

About Antigua and Barbuda

Antigua and Barbuda, nestled in the heart of the Caribbean, is a sovereign island nation that boasts a rich tapestry of history, culture, and natural beauty. Comprising two major islands, Antigua and Barbuda, along with several smaller isles like Great Bird and Redonda, this picturesque country offers a captivating blend of landscapes and experiences.

Discovered by Christopher Columbus in 1493, Antigua derives its name from the Church of Santa María La Antigua, a testament to its storied past. Colonized by Great Britain in the 17th century, the islands became integral parts of the British Empire's colonial legacy. Today, St. John's, Antigua's vibrant capital, stands as a bustling hub of activity, while Codrington serves as the largest town on Barbuda.

In 1981, Antigua and Barbuda proudly declared independence from the United Kingdom, marking a pivotal moment in their history. As a member of the Commonwealth, the nation embraces a constitutional monarchy, with Charles III as its esteemed head of state.

With its economy primarily driven by tourism, Antigua and Barbuda beckon travelers with sun-drenched beaches, azure waters, and a wealth of outdoor adventures. From snorkeling in Stingray City to exploring the historic Nelson's Dockyard, each corner of the islands offers a new discovery.

Yet, like many island nations, Antigua and Barbuda face challenges posed by climate change, including rising sea levels and extreme weather events. Despite these obstacles, the resilience and spirit of its people shine through, forging a path toward sustainable development and environmental stewardship.

Antigua and Barbuda also extend a warm invitation to global citizens through its citizenship by investment program, while its tax-friendly policies make it an attractive destination for investors and expatriates alike.

As you delve into the enchanting world of Antigua and Barbuda, prepare to be captivated by its charm, inspired by its history, and rejuvenated by its natural wonders. Embrace the magic, embrace the warmth, and let the spirit of Antigua and Barbuda forever reside in your heart.

Reasons to Love Antigua and Barbuda

In the heart of the Caribbean, where the sun kisses the shores and history whispers through the trade winds, Antigua and Barbuda emerge as a tapestry of wonder and warmth. From pristine beaches to vibrant local culture, there's something about these islands that captures the soul. Here are the reasons why you'll undoubtedly fall in love:

Breathtaking Beaches: Imagine sinking your toes into powdery white sand, with the crystal-clear waters of the Caribbean lapping at the shore. Antigua's beaches, from Jumby Bay to Devil's Bridge, redefine paradise.

Historic Charm: Wander through the cobblestone streets of Nelson's Dockyard, a living testament to Antigua's maritime legacy. Each brick holds stories of the past, inviting you to step into history.

Underwater Wonders: Snorkel with graceful stingrays in the mesmerizing Stingray City. The vibrant marine life and coral reefs create an aquatic wonderland beneath the surface.

Tranquil Barbuda: Escape to the untouched beauty of Barbuda, where pink sand beaches and a serene atmosphere redefine relaxation. Barbuda Belle becomes your haven, and the Frigate Bird Sanctuary a tranquil escape.

Sunday Bliss at Shirley Heights: Let reggae tunes serenade you as you savor jerk chicken at Shirley Heights Lookout. The panoramic views of English Harbour and the Caribbean Sea make Sundays a celebration.

Local Flavors: Indulge in the delectable local cuisine, from savory rotis at the Roti King to fresh seafood markets bursting with flavor. Your taste buds are in for a treat.

Nature's Spectacle: Witness the majesty of frigate birds soaring in the Codrington Lagoon. Barbuda's untouched landscapes and the natural wonder of Devil's Bridge will leave you in awe.

Warmth of the People: The true magic lies in the smiles and warmth of the locals. Embrace the vibrant culture, connect with the community, and let the spirit of Antigua and Barbuda captivate you.

As you embark on this Caribbean escapade, be prepared to fall head over heels for the enchanting charm of Antigua and Barbuda. Each moment is an invitation to love, to explore, and to create memories that linger long after the sun has set over the turquoise horizon.

History and Culture Overview

Antigua and Barbuda's rich history and vibrant culture create a tapestry that tells the story of resilience, exploration, and a fusion of influences. Discovered by Christopher Columbus in 1493, Antigua became a key player in the grand stage of European colonialism. Its name, derived from the Church of Santa María La Antigua, reflects the deep roots of its Spanish connection.

Fast forward to the 17th century, and the islands found themselves under the colonial embrace of Great Britain. This era left an indelible mark, visible in the cobblestone streets and colonial architecture of places like Nelson's Dockyard. The dockyard, a UNESCO World Heritage Site, stands as a living monument to Antigua's maritime history, echoing tales of naval strategy and trade.

Barbuda, Antigua's tranquil sister, carries a quieter history. It became a haven for enslaved individuals who sought refuge during the colonization era. Today, Barbuda's landscapes remain untouched, a testament to the resilience of its people and the simplicity that defines its charm.

Independence came to Antigua and Barbuda in 1981, marking a turning point in their narrative. As a member of the Commonwealth with a constitutional monarchy, the islands hold a unique position in the modern geopolitical landscape.

Yet, beyond the historical narratives, it's the cultural heartbeat that truly defines these islands. From the vibrant beats of local music to the colorful markets brimming with handmade crafts, Antigua and Barbuda celebrate a lively culture. Festivals like Carnival and the Antigua Sailing Week embody the spirit of celebration and community, inviting visitors to join in the rhythm of life.

As you explore the shores and streets of Antigua and Barbuda, every step becomes a journey through time and a celebration of the resilience and diversity that shape these beautiful islands. The history and culture here are not confined to textbooks but are alive in the smiles of the locals, the melodies of the music, and the stories whispered by the wind.

CHAPTER 1: PLANNING YOUR TRIP TO ANTIGUA AND BARBUDA

Planning your trip to Antigua and Barbuda is an exciting journey that begins with timing your visit just right. With its tropical climate, the islands offer year-round sunshine, but the peak tourist season typically falls between December and April when the weather is drier and cooler. However, if you're looking for fewer crowds and lower prices, consider visiting during the shoulder seasons of May to November, despite the possibility of occasional showers.

Getting to Antigua and Barbuda is relatively easy, thanks to its well-connected international airport in St. John's. Direct flights are available from major cities in North America, Europe, and the Caribbean, making it accessible to travelers from around the world. Once you arrive, getting around the islands is convenient with various transportation options like taxis, rental cars, and public buses, allowing you to explore at your own pace.

Choosing the right accommodation is crucial for a comfortable stay, and Antigua and Barbuda offer a range of options to suit every preference and budget. From luxury resorts in bustling neighborhoods to cozy guesthouses tucked away in serene corners, there's something for everyone. When packing for your trip, don't forget essentials like sunscreen, beachwear, and insect repellent, along with light clothing and comfortable shoes for exploring the islands' diverse landscapes.

As you plan your trip, be sure to check entry and visa requirements for your nationality, ensuring a smooth arrival. The official currency is the Eastern Caribbean Dollar (XCD), but US dollars are widely accepted. English is the official language spoken on the islands, making communication easy for English speakers. To make the most of your budget, consider setting aside funds for activities and dining experiences, and explore money-saving tips like opting for local eateries and booking accommodations in advance through reputable platforms.

When to Visit Antigua and Barbuda

Antigua and Barbuda, blessed with a tropical climate, beckon travelers year-round with the promise of sun-soaked days and balmy nights. The islands experience two distinct seasons - the dry season from December to April and the wet season from May to November. The dry season, with its lower humidity and cooler temperatures, is considered the peak tourist period. However, the wet season, though marked by sporadic showers, unveils lush landscapes and fewer crowds.

The Dry Season: December to April
From December to April, Antigua and Barbuda don their sunniest attire, attracting visitors seeking idyllic beach days and outdoor adventures. During this period, temperatures hover between 75°F to 85°F (24°C to 29°C), creating the perfect climate for snorkeling in Stingray City or exploring historic sites like Nelson's Dockyard. The clear skies and gentle breezes make it an ideal time for sailing enthusiasts to navigate the azure waters.

The Wet Season: May to November
While the wet season may shy some travelers away, it unveils a different side of the islands. From May to November, occasional showers bring the landscapes to life, painting them in vibrant shades of green. Temperatures rise slightly, ranging from 77°F to 88°F (25°C to 31°C), creating a more humid environment. This period is perfect for budget-conscious travelers, as accommodation prices tend to dip, and the islands are less crowded.

Special Considerations: Hurricane Season
It's important to note that the wet season coincides with the hurricane season, officially from June to November. While the

probability of a direct hit is relatively low, it's wise to keep an eye on weather forecasts, especially in the peak months of August and September. Despite this, many travelers find the shoulder seasons of May and November to strike a sweet balance between favorable weather, affordability, and a more tranquil atmosphere.

Whether you prefer the sun-drenched days of the dry season or the lush landscapes of the wet season, Antigua and Barbuda await, offering a tropical escape tailored to your preferred time of visit.

How to Get to Antigua and Barbuda

Getting to the enchanting islands of Antigua and Barbuda is a seamless journey, offering various transportation options to suit your preferences and travel style. The main point of entry is the V.C. Bird International Airport in St. John's, Antigua, which is well-connected to major cities worldwide.

By Air: Direct Flights to V.C. Bird International Airport
For international travelers, reaching Antigua and Barbuda often involves direct flights. The V.C. Bird International Airport welcomes flights from North America, Europe, and the Caribbean, making it accessible from diverse corners of the globe. Airlines like American Airlines, British Airways, Delta, and Caribbean Airlines regularly operate routes to and from Antigua, ensuring a convenient and well-connected air travel experience.

By Sea: Cruising Into Paradise
Another picturesque way to arrive is by sea, particularly if you're on a Caribbean cruise adventure. St. John's, the capital of Antigua, serves as a popular port of call for cruise ships, allowing passengers to disembark and explore the island's attractions. This maritime arrival offers a breathtaking introduction to the coastal beauty that awaits on both Antigua and Barbuda.

Inter-Island Travel: Navigating Between Antigua and Barbuda
Once in Antigua, if you desire to explore its serene sister island, Barbuda, you can hop on a short flight from V.C. Bird International Airport or take a ferry from St. John's. The journey is quick and provides stunning aerial or maritime views, adding an extra layer of excitement to your island-hopping adventure.

Whether you choose the convenience of air travel, the scenic route of a cruise, or the thrill of inter-island exploration, the journey to Antigua and Barbuda sets the stage for an unforgettable Caribbean experience. With multiple options at your disposal, your path to paradise is as diverse as the beauty that awaits upon your arrival.

Getting Around in Antigua and Barbuda

Navigating the captivating landscapes of Antigua and Barbuda is a breeze, thanks to the variety of transportation options available on these picturesque islands. From leisurely strolls through historic sites to adventurous drives along the coastline, getting around ensures you don't miss a moment of the tropical charm.

Taxis: Comfortable and Convenient
Taxis are a popular and convenient mode of transportation for exploring both Antigua and Barbuda. Found at key points like the airport and major hotels, taxis provide a comfortable and hassle-free way to reach your destination. Ensure you agree on the fare with the driver before setting off, as some taxis may not have meters.

Rental Cars: Freedom to Roam
For those seeking independence and flexibility, renting a car is an excellent choice. Several car rental agencies operate on the islands, offering a range of vehicles to suit different preferences. Driving is on the left side of the road, and the well-maintained road network makes it easy to explore at your own pace. Keep in mind that a valid driver's license from your home country is required.

Public Buses: Affordable and Scenic
Public buses, known as "bus vans," provide an affordable way to travel between towns and neighborhoods in Antigua. They are recognizable by their vibrant colors and are a great option for those looking to experience local life. Keep in mind that bus schedules may vary, so it's advisable to check in advance.

Water Taxis: Island-Hopping Adventures
To transition seamlessly between Antigua and Barbuda or explore coastal wonders, consider taking a water taxi. These vessels offer a scenic and swift journey, providing stunning views of the islands from the water. It's a unique experience that adds an extra layer of excitement to your island exploration.

Getting around in Antigua and Barbuda is a delightful part of the adventure via any of the available transportation means. Embrace the laid-back Caribbean pace and let each mode of transport unveil a new facet of these tropical gems.

Where to Stay: Neighbourhoods in Antigua and Barbuda

Antigua and Barbuda offer a variety of neighborhoods and accommodations to suit every traveler's preferences, whether you're seeking bustling city life or tranquil seaside retreats.

St. John's: Vibrant Capital Hub
St. John's, the capital of Antigua, serves as a bustling hub with a range of accommodation options to choose from. The historic Redcliffe Quay and Heritage Quay are located in the heart of the city, offering charming boutique hotels and guesthouses nestled among vibrant shops and restaurants. Don't miss exploring the colorful Saturday morning market, where you can immerse yourself in the local culture and find unique souvenirs.

English Harbour: Historic Charm
Located on the southern coast of Antigua, English Harbour is renowned for its historic Nelson's Dockyard, a UNESCO World Heritage Site. The area boasts upscale resorts and boutique hotels, such as The Admiral's Inn and The Copper and Lumber Store Hotel, housed within restored colonial buildings. Visitors can enjoy stunning views of the harbor, explore the dockyard's maritime history, and dine at waterfront restaurants offering fresh seafood delicacies.

Dickenson Bay: Beachfront Bliss
For those seeking sun, sand, and sea, Dickenson Bay is a popular choice. Situated on the northwest coast of Antigua, this area features luxurious beachfront resorts like Sandals Grande Antigua Resort & Spa and Dickenson Bay Cottages. Visitors can

indulge in water sports, relax on pristine white sands, and enjoy breathtaking sunset views over the Caribbean Sea.

Barbuda: Tranquil Escapes
Across the channel lies the serene island of Barbuda, known for its untouched natural beauty and secluded retreats. Barbuda Belle, nestled on the northwestern coast, offers exclusive beachfront villas and eco-luxury experiences. Visitors can explore the Frigate Bird Sanctuary, relax on the pink sand beaches of Princess Diana Beach, and immerse themselves in the tranquility of island life.

From historic landmarks to pristine beaches, each neighborhood presents its own unique charm and attractions, ensuring a memorable stay in the Caribbean paradise.

What to Pack for Your Antigua and Barbuda Adventure

Embarking on your Caribbean getaway to Antigua and Barbuda requires strategic packing to ensure you're well-prepared for the sun-soaked adventures and diverse activities these islands offer.

Sun Protection Essentials:
With the tropical sun overhead, packing sun protection is a must. Include high SPF sunscreen, a wide-brimmed hat, and UV-blocking sunglasses to shield yourself during beach outings and outdoor explorations.

Beachwear and Lightweight Clothing:
Pack your favorite swimsuits, cover-ups, and beach attire for the countless hours you'll spend basking in the sun. Lightweight, breathable clothing is essential for exploring the islands' diverse landscapes and keeping cool in the warm climate.

Comfortable Footwear:
Whether you're strolling through historic sites, hiking nature trails, or sinking your toes into the sands of pristine beaches, comfortable footwear is key. Include sandals, sneakers, and water shoes to cater to various activities.

Insect Repellent:
Antigua and Barbuda's tropical climate means you may encounter some mosquitoes. To ward off any unwanted pests, pack a reliable insect repellent to keep your island adventures itch-free.

Snorkeling Gear:
For those planning to explore the underwater wonders, consider bringing your snorkeling gear. While many resorts and tour operators provide equipment, having your own ensures a personalized and comfortable experience.

Electronics and Chargers:
Don't forget your camera or smartphone to capture the breathtaking landscapes and vibrant culture. Pack chargers and adapters to keep your devices powered throughout your stay.

Light Rain Gear:
If you're visiting during the wet season, a compact rain jacket or poncho can come in handy for unexpected showers. This ensures you're prepared while still enjoying the beauty of the islands.

Reusable Water Bottle:
Staying hydrated is crucial in the Caribbean sun. Bring a reusable water bottle to refill throughout the day, especially if you're exploring outdoors.

Travel Documents and Essentials:
Ensure you have your passport, travel insurance, and any necessary documents for entry. Keep copies of important information in a separate bag as a precaution.

By packing smart and considering the diverse activities these islands offer, you'll be well-equipped to make the most of your Antigua and Barbuda adventure. Tailor your suitcase to the Caribbean lifestyle, and get ready for a vacation filled with sun, sea, and unforgettable moments.

Entry and Visa Requirements

Planning your entry to the enchanting islands of Antigua and Barbuda involves a straightforward process, ensuring a smooth start to your Caribbean adventure.

Visa Requirements:
For many travelers, the good news is that Antigua and Barbuda generally have liberal visa policies. Citizens of several countries, including the United States, Canada, the United Kingdom, and European Union member states, typically enjoy visa-free entry for stays of up to 90 days. However, it's crucial to check specific visa requirements based on your nationality, as some travelers may need to obtain a visa in advance.

Passport Validity:
Ensure your passport is valid for at least six months beyond your intended departure date from Antigua and Barbuda. Having a valid passport is a standard requirement for entry, and it's wise to check its expiration well before your planned travel dates.

Onward or Return Ticket:
Immigration authorities often require visitors to show proof of onward or return travel. Have a copy of your return ticket or a confirmed itinerary readily available for inspection upon arrival. This ensures compliance with the entry regulations and helps facilitate a swift entry process.

Customs Declaration:
Upon arrival, you'll need to complete a customs declaration form. Be accurate and transparent in declaring any items you're bringing into the country. Antigua and Barbuda have regulations

regarding duty-free allowances, and adherence to these guidelines ensures a hassle-free experience.

Vaccination Requirements:
As of the latest information available, Antigua and Barbuda generally do not have specific vaccination requirements for entry. However, it's always wise to check for any updates or changes in regulations closer to your travel dates.

Ensuring you meet these entry requirements sets the stage for a seamless arrival, allowing you to dive into the beauty and warmth of Antigua and Barbuda without any unnecessary delays. Remember to double-check entry requirements based on your nationality and stay updated on any changes before you embark on your Caribbean escape.

Currency and Language

Understanding the local currency and language is essential for a seamless experience while exploring the vibrant culture and stunning landscapes of Antigua and Barbuda.

The official currency of Antigua and Barbuda is the Eastern Caribbean Dollar (XCD). While the US dollar is widely accepted across the islands, it's advisable to carry some Eastern Caribbean Dollars for smaller transactions and purchases in local markets. Currency exchange services are available at the airport, banks, and authorized exchange bureaus throughout the islands.

English is the official language spoken in Antigua and Barbuda, making communication easy and accessible for travelers from English-speaking countries.

The local dialect, known as Antiguan Creole, is also spoken by some residents and adds to the colorful tapestry of language on the islands. Visitors will find that most locals are fluent in English, making interactions and navigating daily life a breeze.

As you immerse yourself in the vibrant culture and warm hospitality of Antigua and Barbuda, having a basic understanding of the local currency and language enhances your travel experience. Whether you're exploring historic sites, relaxing on pristine beaches, or sampling local cuisine, embracing the currency and language of the islands enriches your Caribbean adventure.

Suggested Budget

Antigua and Barbuda, with its sun-drenched beaches and diverse activities, cater to a range of budgets, allowing you to tailor your Caribbean adventure to your preferences. Here's a breakdown of a suggested budget to help you plan your memorable stay in these tropical paradises.

Accommodation:
Accommodation options vary from budget-friendly guesthouses to luxurious resorts. Budget travelers can find comfortable stays for around $50 to $150 per night, while mid-range options range from $150 to $300. Upscale resorts and boutique hotels can go beyond $300 per night, offering indulgent amenities and breathtaking views.

Dining:
Dining in Antigua and Barbuda offers diverse options, from local eateries to fine dining establishments. On average, a meal at a mid-range restaurant may cost between $20 to $50 per person, while street food and casual dining options are more budget-friendly, ranging from $5 to $20. For those who enjoy cooking or want to save on meals, local markets offer fresh produce at reasonable prices.

Transportation:
Transportation costs depend on your preferred mode of travel. Taxis are convenient but can be relatively expensive, with fares starting at $20. Renting a car provides flexibility, with daily rates ranging from $50 to $100. Public buses offer an affordable option, with fares averaging around $2 to $5. If you plan to explore both Antigua and Barbuda, consider budgeting for inter-island flights or ferry rides.

Activities and Excursions:
Antigua and Barbuda offer a plethora of activities, from guided tours to water sports. Excursion prices vary, with activities like snorkeling and boat tours ranging from $50 to $150 per person. Entrance fees to attractions such as Nelson's Dockyard or Shirley Heights Lookout may cost around $10 to $30.

Miscellaneous:
Include a buffer for miscellaneous expenses, such as souvenirs, sunscreen, and any unforeseen costs. A daily budget of $20 to $50 should cover incidentals and allow for spontaneity during your stay.

Total Daily Budget:
Budget Traveler: $100 to $200 per day
Mid-Range Traveler: $200 to $400 per day
Luxury Traveler: $400 and above per day

Tailor your budget based on your preferences and priorities, allowing flexibility for spontaneous experiences and unique adventures. Antigua and Barbuda welcome all budgets, ensuring that every traveler can create lasting memories in this Caribbean haven.

Money-Saving Tips

Exploring the sun-soaked landscapes and vibrant culture of Antigua and Barbuda doesn't have to break the bank. With a few savvy strategies, you can make the most of your Caribbean adventure while keeping your budget in check. Here are some money-saving tips to consider:

1. Travel During the Off-Season:
Consider visiting Antigua and Barbuda during the shoulder seasons (May to November) when accommodation prices tend to be lower, and crowds are thinner. You'll still enjoy the tropical climate and stunning scenery while saving on accommodation and activity costs.

2. Take Advantage of Happy Hours and Specials:
Many restaurants and bars offer happy hour specials and discounts on food and drinks during certain times of the day. Take advantage of these promotions to indulge in delicious cuisine and refreshing beverages without breaking the bank.

3. Explore Free and Low-Cost Activities:
Antigua and Barbuda offer a wealth of free and low-cost activities, from hiking scenic trails to lounging on pristine beaches. Take advantage of nature's wonders and explore attractions like Devil's Bridge, Darkwood Beach, and local markets without spending a dime.

4. Opt for Local Eateries and Street Food:
Dining at local eateries and sampling street food is not only budget-friendly but also an excellent way to experience authentic Antiguan and Barbudan cuisine. Look for roadside stalls and small restaurants serving delicious dishes at affordable prices.

5. Use Public Transportation:
Public buses, known as "bus vans," provide an affordable way to travel between towns and attractions in Antigua. Opt for public transportation instead of taxis to save money on getting around the island.

6. Look for Accommodation Deals:
Keep an eye out for accommodation deals and promotions offered by hotels and resorts in Antigua and Barbuda. Booking in advance or during off-peak periods can often result in significant savings on room rates.

7. Bring Your Snorkeling Gear:
If you plan to snorkel during your visit, consider bringing your gear to avoid rental fees. Many beaches in Antigua and Barbuda offer excellent snorkeling opportunities, allowing you to explore colorful coral reefs and marine life without additional costs.

By incorporating these money-saving tips into your travel plans, you can enjoy all that Antigua and Barbuda have to offer while staying within your budget. Embrace the spirit of adventure and discovery, knowing that you're making smart choices that allow you to experience the Caribbean's beauty without breaking the bank.

Best Places to Book Your Trip

Embarking on your Antigua and Barbuda journey starts with choosing the right platforms for booking flights, accommodations, and activities. Here are some trusted websites to streamline your travel plans:

1. Expedia (www.expedia.com):
For comprehensive travel packages that include flights, hotels, and car rentals, Expedia is a go-to platform. The user-friendly interface allows you to customize your itinerary and find deals that suit your budget. Explore a variety of accommodation options and discover special promotions for a cost-effective Caribbean getaway.

2. Booking.com (www.booking.com):
Booking.com is renowned for its extensive selection of accommodations worldwide. Whether you're seeking beachfront resorts, boutique hotels, or budget-friendly guesthouses, this platform provides a diverse range of options. Transparent reviews from fellow travelers help you make informed decisions, ensuring a comfortable stay.

3. Airbnb (www.airbnb.com):
For a more personalized and local experience, Airbnb offers a variety of rental options, including apartments, villas, and private rooms. Connect with hosts who provide insights into the local culture, making your stay in Antigua and Barbuda more immersive and memorable.

4. Skyscanner (www.skyscanner.com):
When it comes to finding the best flight deals, Skyscanner is a valuable resource. Compare prices from various airlines and

travel agencies to secure affordable airfare. The platform's flexible date feature helps you identify the most budget-friendly times to fly to Antigua and Barbuda.

5. Viator (www.viator.com):
To enhance your Caribbean experience with exciting activities and tours, Viator is an excellent choice. Browse through a multitude of tours, excursions, and adventure options in Antigua and Barbuda. Booking in advance not only ensures availability but often comes with discounted rates.

6. TripAdvisor (www.tripadvisor.com):
For reliable reviews and insights from fellow travelers, TripAdvisor is an invaluable resource. Explore hotel and restaurant reviews, discover hidden gems, and gain insider tips to make the most of your Antigua and Barbuda adventure. The platform's forums can also provide answers to specific travel queries.

These platforms offer a seamless and convenient way to plan your Antigua and Barbuda getaway. From flights to accommodations and activities, utilizing these trusted websites ensures a smooth and enjoyable travel experience in the Caribbean.

CHAPTER 2: MUST-SEE ATTRACTIONS AND LANDMARKS

As you delve into the heart of Antigua and Barbuda, a treasure trove of captivating attractions and landmarks awaits, each weaving a tale of history, natural beauty, and Caribbean charm. Begin your exploration at Nelson's Dockyard, a UNESCO World Heritage Site nestled in English Harbour. This historic naval yard, named after Admiral Horatio Nelson, is a testament to the islands' maritime legacy, showcasing restored colonial-era buildings and serving as a hub for vibrant events and cultural experiences.

Perched above Nelson's Dockyard, the panoramic vista from Shirley Heights offers an awe-inspiring backdrop. This elevated vantage point, historically used for military purposes, now stands as a social hub for locals and visitors alike. Sundays come alive with lively gatherings, live music, and the breathtaking spectacle of a Caribbean sunset, making it a must-visit spot for both history enthusiasts and those seeking a festive atmosphere.

Venture to Devil's Bridge, a natural limestone arch carved by the relentless Atlantic waves. This geological wonder, steeped in local folklore, invites contemplation of the forces that shaped the islands. Continue your journey to St. John's Cathedral, a striking architectural gem in the heart of the capital. This Anglican cathedral, with its white towers piercing the sky, stands as a symbol of spiritual resilience and offers a serene escape within the bustling city.

From the historical to the natural wonders, Antigua and Barbuda beckon you to explore Betty's Hope, a restored sugar plantation dating back to the 17th century. As you meander through the lush surroundings, feel the echoes of the island's sugar-producing past. For sun-soaked relaxation, Darkwood Beach, with its pristine sands and crystal-clear waters, provides an idyllic retreat.

The islands also offer thrilling adventures, such as the Antigua Rainforest Canopy Tour, where ziplining through the lush green canopy provides an adrenaline rush against a backdrop of tropical splendor. And if it's tranquility you seek, the untouched beauty of Great Bird Island and the historic ambiance of Fort James provide diverse experiences for every traveler.

As you uncover these must-see attractions and landmarks, each corner of Antigua and Barbuda reveals a unique chapter in the story of these enchanting islands. From the heights of Shirley Heights to the depths of Devil's Bridge, your journey promises a kaleidoscope of experiences that capture the essence of the Caribbean spirit.

Nelson's Dockyard

Nelson's Dockyard, a historical gem nestled in English Harbour, stands as a testament to Antigua and Barbuda's rich maritime heritage. This UNESCO World Heritage Site, named after the legendary Admiral Horatio Nelson, showcases meticulously restored naval structures dating back to the 18th century. Addressing the maritime needs of the British Royal Navy during the Caribbean colonial era, the dockyard has become an iconic symbol of the islands' historical significance.

Situated on the southern tip of Antigua, reaching Nelson's Dockyard is a scenic journey. Located at English Harbour, the dockyard is approximately 19 kilometers (12 miles) from the capital city, St. John's. Traveling by car provides a picturesque drive, offering glimpses of the island's coastal beauty. If you prefer a more leisurely approach, consider taking a boat tour that allows you to appreciate the historical site from the turquoise waters surrounding it.

Upon arriving at Nelson's Dockyard, you step into a living museum of maritime history. Explore the Admiral's Inn and the Copper and Lumber Store Hotel, both housed in restored colonial buildings, providing an immersive experience of the dockyard's past. The Naval Officer's House, now the Dockyard Museum, offers a fascinating collection of artifacts, maps, and exhibits that unravel the stories of the dockyard's heyday.

Beyond the historical structures, Nelson's Dockyard buzzes with vibrant life. The marina is a hub for yachts and sailing enthusiasts, creating a lively atmosphere. Visitors can stroll along the charming cobblestone streets, lined with boutiques, galleries, and restaurants. Indulge in local cuisine at one of the waterfront eateries, savoring the fusion of Caribbean flavors and maritime ambiance.

For those seeking a deeper connection with the dockyard's past, a visit to the Pillars of Hercules, the stone pillars marking the entrance, provides a poignant view of the naval history that unfolded within these shores. Nelson's Dockyard is not merely a static historical site; it breathes life into the tales of seafaring adventures and the resilience of a bygone era, making it a must-visit destination for history enthusiasts and curious travelers alike.

Shirley Heights

Perched atop the lush hills overlooking English Harbour, Shirley Heights offers an enchanting panorama of Antigua and Barbuda's coastal beauty. This elevated vantage point, historically significant for military purposes, has transformed into a cultural and social hub that beckons both locals and visitors seeking a captivating experience.

Located on the southern part of Antigua, Shirley Heights is easily accessible from English Harbour, approximately 18 kilometers (11 miles) from the capital, St. John's. The journey to this elevated lookout unfolds through winding roads, revealing glimpses of the island's natural splendor. Whether by car or as part of an organized tour, the ascent to Shirley Heights promises scenic vistas and a sense of anticipation.

Sundays at Shirley Heights are particularly renowned for the lively atmosphere and spectacular sunsets. A weekly tradition, the Shirley Heights Lookout Party welcomes locals and tourists alike to revel in the Caribbean spirit. Live music fills the air as local bands play a medley of reggae, steel drum melodies, and soca tunes. The festive ambiance, combined with the scent of local cuisine wafting from the barbecue grills, creates an unforgettable experience.

Beyond the Sunday soirées, Shirley Heights offers daytime tranquility and exploration. The historic military complex showcases remnants of military structures, including the restored gun platforms that once guarded English Harbour. Visitors can wander through these historical sites, absorbing the stories etched into the stones and enjoying breathtaking vistas of the coastline and neighboring islands.

Hiking trails surround Shirley Heights, allowing more adventurous explorers to venture into the surrounding hills and soak in the natural beauty. Whether you're captivated by the historical remnants or lured by the lively Sunday gatherings, Shirley Heights invites you to experience Antigua and Barbuda from a perspective that combines history, culture, and the sheer beauty of the Caribbean landscape.

Devil's Bridge

In the wild and rugged eastern coast of Antigua, Devil's Bridge stands as a captivating natural wonder carved by the relentless forces of the Atlantic Ocean. This unique limestone arch, named for the turbulent waters that crash against the rocks, showcases the power of nature and offers visitors a mesmerizing spectacle.

Located on the eastern tip of Antigua, Devil's Bridge is a roughly 30-minute drive from the capital, St. John's. Navigating the island's winding roads to reach this geological marvel provides a scenic journey through diverse landscapes. The journey is an opportunity to appreciate the island's rugged beauty before arriving at the striking coastal site.

As you approach Devil's Bridge, the dramatic coastline unfolds, revealing the majestic arch rising from the tumultuous waves below. The natural bridge, formed over centuries by the relentless erosion of the limestone rocks, allows visitors to witness the unyielding clash between the Atlantic Ocean and the Caribbean Sea. The churning waters and breathtaking views create a serene yet powerful ambiance that resonates with the island's untamed allure.

Beyond its geological significance, Devil's Bridge is steeped in local folklore. According to legend, slaves once leaped off the bridge to escape the harsh conditions of plantation life, choosing the uncertain depths below over the hardships above. This poignant history adds layers of meaning to the site, creating a place of both natural beauty and historical reflection.

Visitors to Devil's Bridge can explore the surrounding area, where tide pools form intricate patterns in the rocks, and the coastal terrain provides a picturesque backdrop for photography. While the natural allure of Devil's Bridge is evident throughout the day, sunrise and sunset visits offer a particularly magical experience, as the changing light accentuates the dramatic contours of the landscape.

Devil's Bridge invites you to witness the raw beauty of Antigua's eastern coast, where nature's forces have sculpted a masterpiece in stone. It's a place where the Caribbean's serene charm meets the untamed energy of the Atlantic, creating an unforgettable tableau of natural drama.

St. John's Cathedral

In the heart of Antigua's capital city, St. John's Cathedral stands as a testament to the island's rich religious heritage and architectural grandeur. This Anglican cathedral, with its pristine white towers piercing the sky, serves as a beacon of faith and a symbol of resilience for the local community and visitors alike.

Situated in the bustling downtown area of St. John's, the cathedral's location makes it easily accessible to both residents and tourists exploring the city. Its prominent position amidst the vibrant streets and bustling markets underscores its significance as a spiritual and cultural landmark in Antigua.

Stepping inside St. John's Cathedral, visitors are greeted by a serene ambiance and the majestic beauty of its interior. The cathedral's elegant Gothic architecture, adorned with intricate stained glass windows and ornate furnishings, reflects centuries of devotion and craftsmanship.

As one of the oldest Anglican cathedrals in the Caribbean, St. John's Cathedral carries a rich history dating back to its construction in the 17th century. Over the years, the cathedral has withstood the test of time and weathered numerous hurricanes and natural disasters, serving as a resilient symbol of faith and endurance for the local community.

Beyond its architectural splendor, St. John's Cathedral serves as a place of worship, offering solace and spiritual guidance to those who seek it. Regular services and special events held within its hallowed halls provide opportunities for reflection, prayer, and communion for residents and visitors alike.

For those exploring the city of St. John's, a visit to the cathedral offers a glimpse into Antigua's religious and cultural heritage. Whether admiring its majestic facade from the outside or exploring its sacred interior, St. John's Cathedral invites visitors to experience the timeless beauty and spiritual significance of this iconic landmark in the heart of Antigua's capital.

Betty's Hope

Nestled in the lush landscapes of Antigua, Betty's Hope stands as a poignant reminder of the island's historical ties to sugar cultivation and the resilience of its people. This former sugar plantation, dating back to the 17th century, provides visitors with a captivating journey into Antigua's agricultural past and the complex legacy of its colonial history.

Located in the eastern part of the island, Betty's Hope is easily accessible, situated approximately 16 kilometers (10 miles) from the capital, St. John's. The journey to this historical site offers scenic views of Antigua's countryside, providing a tranquil backdrop that contrasts with the bustling urban center.

As you explore Betty's Hope, the well-preserved remnants of the sugar estate unfold before you. The iconic stone windmill towers, remnants of the original sugar mill, stand as silent witnesses to the once-thriving industry that shaped Antigua's economic landscape. The surrounding grounds feature the ruins of the estate's great house, outbuildings, and the slave quarters, offering a poignant glimpse into the harsh realities of plantation life.

A visit to the Betty's Hope Interpretation Centre enhances the experience, providing insightful exhibits that detail the plantation's history, the process of sugar production, and the lives of the enslaved individuals who toiled on the estate. The center serves as an educational hub, shedding light on the complex layers of Antigua's past.

Beyond its historical significance, Betty's Hope is embraced by nature, with the surrounding fields and landscapes offering a peaceful retreat. Visitors can stroll through the grounds, taking in the serenity of the site and reflecting on the historical narratives embedded in its foundations.

Betty's Hope encapsulates the bittersweet history of Antigua's sugar industry, from its prosperous beginnings to the challenging legacies it left behind. The site invites exploration and contemplation, allowing visitors to connect with the island's past while surrounded by the tranquil beauty of its present-day setting.

Darkwood Beach

Darkwood Beach, situated on the southwestern coast of Antigua, beckons with its pristine sands and crystal-clear waters, creating an idyllic haven for those seeking a tranquil retreat. Located near Johnson's Point, accessing Darkwood Beach is a straightforward journey, approximately 17 kilometers (10.5 miles) from the capital, St. John's. Whether by car or taxi, the drive unveils picturesque views, providing a glimpse of the island's coastal charm.

Upon arrival at Darkwood Beach, visitors are greeted by a crescent of soft, golden sand framed by lush greenery. The beach's calm, turquoise waters invite leisurely swims and moments of relaxation. The absence of large crowds enhances the beach's peaceful ambiance, allowing for a serene escape from the bustle of everyday life.

Shaded areas with palm trees and sea grapes offer spots to unwind and enjoy the gentle Caribbean breeze. Beachgoers can spread out on the soft sand or set up a cozy spot beneath the natural canopy, creating a perfect environment for picnics or simply soaking up the sun. The laid-back atmosphere makes Darkwood Beach a favorite among locals and tourists alike, seeking a quiet oasis away from the more bustling shores.

The coral reefs just off the shore provide opportunities for snorkeling, allowing visitors to explore the vibrant underwater world teeming with marine life. Snorkeling gear can often be rented on-site, adding an adventurous dimension to your beach day. For those craving a taste of local flavors, nearby vendors may offer delicious Caribbean snacks and refreshing beverages.

As the sun begins its descent, Darkwood Beach transforms into a romantic setting, offering breathtaking sunset views over the Caribbean Sea. The changing colors of the sky and the tranquil sounds of the waves crashing create a magical atmosphere, making it an ideal spot for a romantic evening or a peaceful end to a day in paradise.

Darkwood Beach, with its unspoiled beauty and serene charm, encapsulates the essence of an idyllic Caribbean escape. Whether you're seeking a quiet retreat, a snorkeling adventure, or a front-row seat to a stunning sunset, Darkwood Beach invites you to unwind and immerse yourself in the natural splendor of Antigua's southwestern coastline.

Antigua Rainforest Canopy Tour

For thrill-seekers and nature enthusiasts, the Antigua Rainforest Canopy Tour promises an exhilarating adventure high above the lush landscapes of the island. Located in the Fig Tree Drive Rainforest, approximately 17 kilometers (10.5 miles) southwest of St. John's, accessing this treetop adventure is a scenic drive through the heart of Antigua's captivating rainforest.

The Antigua Rainforest Canopy Tour invites visitors to embrace the beauty of the island from a unique perspective. The tour features a series of ziplines, suspension bridges, and platforms seamlessly integrated into the rainforest canopy. As you soar through the air, surrounded by the rich biodiversity of the rainforest, the experience becomes a thrilling journey that combines adrenaline-pumping excitement with a deep connection to nature.

Upon arrival, expert guides provide thorough safety briefings and equip participants with the necessary gear, ensuring a secure and enjoyable experience. The ziplines, varying in length and height, allow participants to traverse the rainforest canopy with exhilarating speed, offering panoramic views of the dense foliage, vibrant flora, and glimpses of Antigua's coastline in the distance.

Suspension bridges suspended high above the forest floor provide moments of tranquility, allowing participants to absorb the beauty of the rainforest at a leisurely pace. The tour's eco-friendly approach emphasizes conservation and education, with guides sharing insights about the rainforest's diverse ecosystem and the importance of preserving these natural habitats.

The Antigua Rainforest Canopy Tour is designed to accommodate adventurers of various skill levels, making it an accessible yet thrilling experience for individuals, families, and groups. As you navigate through the treetops, the sounds of tropical birds and the rustling of leaves create a symphony of nature, enhancing the immersive quality of the journey.

Concluding the tour, participants often leave with a profound appreciation for Antigua's ecological treasures. The Antigua Rainforest Canopy Tour offers more than an adrenaline rush; it provides an opportunity to connect with the island's natural splendor in a way that is both invigorating and environmentally conscious.

Half Moon Bay

Half Moon Bay, cradled on the eastern coast of Antigua, unveils a secluded stretch of powdery sand and azure waters, offering an idyllic escape for those in search of tranquility. Located approximately 20 kilometers (12.5 miles) southeast of St. John's, reaching this pristine beach involves a picturesque drive through Antigua's scenic landscapes.

As you approach Half Moon Bay, the captivating crescent-shaped beach comes into view, framed by undulating hills and bordered by lush vegetation. The journey to this hidden gem unfolds through winding roads, creating a sense of anticipation before revealing the unspoiled beauty that awaits.

Half Moon Bay's serene ambiance, characterized by its soft, white sands and clear, calm waters, provides a stark contrast to the more bustling beaches on the island. The absence of large crowds enhances the beach's tranquil charm, creating a haven for those seeking solitude or a quiet day of relaxation.

The gentle waves that lap the shore invite visitors to wade into the refreshing Caribbean Sea or partake in water activities such as swimming and snorkeling. The coral reefs just off the coast teem with marine life, making it an excellent spot for underwater exploration. Snorkeling gear can often be rented nearby, adding an adventurous dimension to your beach day.

For those who prefer to stay ashore, Half Moon Bay offers ample space for sunbathing and picnicking. Shaded areas provided by the surrounding sea grape trees offer refuge from the sun, creating ideal spots for a beachside picnic or simply unwinding with a good book.

Half Moon Bay, with its pristine beauty and unspoiled charm, beckons visitors to savor the simplicity of a day spent amidst nature's splendor. Whether you're drawn to the therapeutic sound of lapping waves or the untouched landscapes that frame the beach, Half Moon Bay invites you to experience the quieter side of Antigua's coastal treasures.

Falmouth Harbor

Falmouth Harbor, nestled on the southern coast of Antigua, serves as a bustling maritime hub and a gateway to the island's rich nautical heritage. Located approximately 20 kilometers (12.5 miles) south of St. John's, accessing Falmouth Harbor offers a scenic drive through Antigua's charming coastal landscapes.

As you approach Falmouth Harbor, the picturesque setting unfolds, revealing a sheltered bay dotted with sailboats, yachts, and historic vessels. The harbor's deep waters and strategic location have made it a preferred destination for sailors and seafarers navigating the Caribbean waters.

Falmouth Harbor is not only a haven for maritime enthusiasts but also a vibrant center of activity, offering an array of waterfront restaurants, shops, and marina services. The lively atmosphere invites visitors to stroll along the docks, where the colorful facades of historic buildings evoke the island's colonial past.

The harbor serves as a launching point for a variety of maritime adventures, from leisurely yacht cruises to exhilarating sailing regattas. Visitors can charter boats for day trips to nearby islands, explore the scenic coastline, or embark on deep-sea fishing excursions in search of prized catches.

Falmouth Harbor is also renowned for its calendar of events, including the annual Antigua Charter Yacht Show and Antigua Sailing Week, which attract sailing enthusiasts and industry professionals from around the world. These events showcase the harbor's vibrant maritime culture and highlight Antigua's reputation as a premier yachting destination.

Beyond its maritime allure, Falmouth Harbor offers breathtaking views of the surrounding hills and coastline, providing a serene backdrop for waterfront dining and sunset gatherings. Whether you're a seasoned sailor or a curious traveler, Falmouth Harbor invites you to immerse yourself in Antigua's maritime legacy and discover the timeless charm of this coastal gem.

Great Bird Island

Great Bird Island, a hidden gem off the northeastern coast of Antigua, beckons nature enthusiasts and seekers of serene landscapes. Located approximately 6 kilometers (3.7 miles) northeast of the capital, St. John's, reaching this pristine island involves a short boat ride, setting the stage for an idyllic escape.

Approaching Great Bird Island, the emerald-green vegetation and the white sandy beaches come into view, creating a captivating contrast against the turquoise waters of the Caribbean Sea. The journey by boat allows visitors to appreciate the untouched beauty of the island's coastline and sets the tone for the tranquility that awaits.

The island's name is derived from the magnificent seabirds that inhabit its shores. Upon landing, visitors are greeted by the sights and sounds of diverse bird species, including frigatebirds and the charming red-billed tropicbirds. Great Bird Island is a designated nature reserve, providing a sanctuary for these avian residents and offering birdwatchers a unique opportunity to observe them in their natural habitat.

The island's relatively small size invites exploration by foot, allowing visitors to meander through well-marked trails that lead to panoramic viewpoints. These vantage points offer stunning views of the surrounding turquoise waters, neighboring islands, and the lush greenery that blankets Great Bird Island.

Snorkeling enthusiasts will find the clear, shallow waters surrounding the island teeming with marine life. The vibrant coral reefs provide a colorful underwater world for snorkelers to explore, making Great Bird Island not only a haven for birdwatchers but also an underwater paradise for those who revel in the beauty beneath the surface.

Great Bird Island is an ideal spot for a day of relaxation, nature appreciation, and aquatic adventure. Whether you're drawn to the call of the seabirds, the vibrant marine life, or the simple pleasure of basking in the sun on a pristine beach, Great Bird Island invites you to savor the untouched beauty of Antigua's northeastern coast.

Fort James

Perched on the northwestern edge of Antigua, Fort James stands as a stoic sentinel, offering a window into the island's military history. Just a short distance from St. John's, the capital, this historic fortification provides not only a strategic vantage point but also a tranquil setting for those seeking a blend of history and scenic views.

As you approach Fort James, the weathered stone walls and aging cannons evoke a sense of the island's colonial past. Built in the early 18th century by the British to protect St. John's Harbor from potential invaders, the fort has witnessed centuries of change and serves as a tangible link to Antigua's maritime heritage.

Exploring Fort James is like stepping back in time. The well-preserved remnants, including the powder magazine and barracks, offer a glimpse into the daily lives of the soldiers who once manned these historic ramparts. The fort's location provides panoramic views of St. John's Harbor and the neighboring coastline, making it a perfect spot for both history enthusiasts and those seeking a quiet place to reflect.

The cannons, still pointing out towards the sea, harken back to an era when maritime defenses were crucial. Today, they serve as silent sentinels, overlooking the tranquil waters and providing a stark contrast to the vibrant hues of the Caribbean Sea.

For visitors, Fort James is not just a historical site but a peaceful haven. The open courtyards and grassy areas invite leisurely strolls, picnics, or moments of quiet contemplation. The sea breeze carries whispers of the past, creating a serene atmosphere that belies the fort's once-military purpose.

As you explore the nooks and crannies of Fort James, the blend of history and natural beauty becomes apparent. It's a place where the stories of the past coexist with the present-day calm, inviting all who visit to appreciate the layers of Antigua's rich history in a setting that embodies both strength and tranquility.

Barbuda's Frigate Bird Sanctuary

Nestled on the island of Barbuda, the Frigate Bird Sanctuary stands as a testament to the incredible biodiversity of the Caribbean. Located on the island's western lagoon, reaching this avian haven involves a short boat ride from Codrington, the main town of Barbuda. The sanctuary's address is a journey through the serene waters that surround the island, providing an opportunity to appreciate the coastal beauty before arriving at this natural spectacle.

Barbuda's Frigate Bird Sanctuary is renowned for hosting one of the largest colonies of magnificent frigatebirds in the Western Hemisphere. These captivating birds, known for their distinctive red throat pouches and impressive wingspans, create a mesmerizing sight as they gracefully soar above the mangrove-lined lagoon. The sanctuary provides a rare opportunity for birdwatchers and nature enthusiasts to witness these magnificent creatures in their natural habitat.

Upon arrival, visitors often embark on guided boat tours, which navigate the labyrinthine waterways to bring observers within close proximity to the nesting colonies. The guided tours not only offer a chance to marvel at the frigatebirds in flight but also provide valuable insights into the ecological importance of the sanctuary and the broader conservation efforts on the island.

Exploring the sanctuary is a sensory experience, with the calls of the frigatebirds echoing through the air. The surrounding mangroves, which serve as crucial nesting grounds, create a serene backdrop for the avian activities. Visitors may also encounter other bird species, such as herons and pelicans, contributing to the sanctuary's status as a haven for diverse birdlife.

Beyond birdwatching, Barbuda's Frigate Bird Sanctuary offers opportunities for photography, as the striking contrast between the red-throated frigatebirds and the lush greenery creates a visually stunning tableau. The sanctuary is not just an excursion into nature but a chance to witness the delicate balance between wildlife conservation and the unique ecosystem of Barbuda.

As you immerse yourself in the sights and sounds of the Frigate Bird Sanctuary, the experience becomes more than a birdwatching adventure; it becomes a journey into the heart of Barbuda's natural wonders, where the avian inhabitants take center stage in this Caribbean oasis.

CHAPTER 3: ACCOMMODATION OPTIONS

Antigua offers a diverse array of accommodation options to suit every traveler's preferences and budget. For those seeking luxury and indulgence, the island boasts a selection of upscale hotels and resorts that redefine the meaning of opulence. From lavish beachfront properties to secluded hillside retreats, these establishments pamper guests with world-class amenities, fine dining experiences, and breathtaking views of the Caribbean Sea.

Travelers on a budget need not compromise on comfort or convenience, as Antigua also offers a range of budget-friendly accommodations. From cozy guesthouses and bed-and-breakfasts to affordable hotels and apartments, there are plenty of options for those looking to stretch their dollar without sacrificing quality. These accommodations provide a welcoming haven for budget-conscious travelers, allowing them to explore the island's attractions while staying within their financial means.

For those seeking a more unique and immersive experience, Antigua boasts a variety of local favorites and hidden gems that offer a taste of authentic Caribbean hospitality. From charming boutique hotels tucked away in historic neighborhoods to eco-friendly lodges nestled amidst lush tropical landscapes, these accommodations provide a glimpse into the island's vibrant culture and heritage. Guests can enjoy personalized service, locally sourced cuisine, and opportunities to connect with the local community.

When booking accommodations in Antigua, practical tips can help travelers make the most of their stay. From booking directly with hotels for special deals and discounts to considering seasonal rates and availability, there are strategies to ensure a smooth and enjoyable experience. Additionally, researching reviews and recommendations from fellow travelers can provide valuable insights into the best places to stay and what to expect during your visit.

With careful planning and consideration, finding the perfect accommodation in Antigua becomes an integral part of the journey, enhancing the overall experience of exploring this captivating Caribbean destination.

Best Luxury Hotels and Resorts

In the lap of luxury, Antigua's finest hotels and resorts beckon travelers to an unparalleled world of opulence and relaxation. These exquisite establishments redefine the art of hospitality, offering a harmonious blend of sophistication, breathtaking surroundings, and impeccable service. Each of these lavish retreats stands as a testament to the island's commitment to providing an extraordinary experience for those seeking the pinnacle of indulgence.

Hermitage Bay Resort: Nestled on the western coast of Antigua, Hermitage Bay Resort captivates with its exclusive hillside villas and pristine beachfront. Accessible through a scenic drive from St. John's, this retreat immerses guests in luxury with private plunge pools, gourmet dining, and panoramic views of the turquoise Caribbean Sea. Activities range from rejuvenating spa treatments to water sports, ensuring an unforgettable stay.

Jumby Bay Island - an Oetker Collection Hotel: Situated on a private island just off Antigua's northeast coast, Jumby Bay Island presents a secluded paradise accessible by a short boat ride. This ultra-luxurious resort boasts lavish suites and private residences surrounded by lush landscapes. With white sandy beaches and clear waters, guests can indulge in watersports, fine dining, and exclusive experiences within the resort's tranquil enclave.

Carlisle Bay Antigua: Located on the island's south coast, Carlisle Bay Antigua offers a blend of contemporary elegance and natural beauty. The resort's beachfront suites and serene ambiance make it a haven for luxury seekers. From yoga on the jetty to exploring nearby rainforests, guests can tailor their experience, creating a perfect balance of relaxation and adventure.

Curtain Bluff Resort: Perched on a picturesque peninsula on the southern tip of Antigua, Curtain Bluff Resort unfolds as a haven of understated luxury. Guests are welcomed with panoramic ocean views and spacious accommodations. With an all-inclusive approach, the resort provides access to various activities, including water sports, tennis, and world-class dining, ensuring a seamless and indulgent escape.

Sandals Grande Antigua Resort and Spa: Situated on Dickenson Bay, Sandals Grande Antigua Resort and Spa is an adults-only haven offering an array of romantic accommodations. With its all-inclusive offerings, this resort invites couples to savor the Caribbean charm with gourmet dining, water activities, and luxurious amenities, providing an intimate retreat for lovebirds.

Each of these luxury establishments in Antigua promises not just accommodation but an immersive journey into the lap of indulgence, where every detail is meticulously curated to create an unforgettable experience for discerning travelers.

Budget-Friendly Accommodations

For the savvy traveler mindful of their budget, Antigua offers a variety of comfortable and cost-effective accommodations without compromising on the island's charm and hospitality. These budget-friendly options provide a welcoming refuge for those seeking to explore Antigua's attractions while ensuring affordability is at the forefront of their travel experience.

Yepton Estate Cottages: Tucked away near Hodges Bay, Yepton Estate Cottages offers a serene escape at an affordable price. The self-catering cottages, surrounded by tropical gardens, provide a homey atmosphere for guests. With a short drive to St. John's and nearby beaches, Yepton Estate Cottages is a convenient and budget-friendly base for exploring Antigua.

Connie's Comfort Suites: Located in the heart of St. John's, Connie's Comfort Suites is a budget-friendly option with a central location. Its proximity to the capital's attractions, markets, and historical sites makes it an ideal choice for those who wish to immerse themselves in the vibrant atmosphere of Antigua without straining their budget.

Cocos Hotel Antigua: Offering a more intimate and affordable experience, Cocos Hotel Antigua is situated on the southwest coast. This boutique resort provides a unique blend of charm and budget-conscious accommodations. Guests can enjoy panoramic sea views, stroll along the resort's private beach, and savor local cuisine at an accessible cost.

Antigua Village Beach Resort: Nestled on Dickenson Bay, Antigua Village Beach Resort offers self-catering accommodations with a budget-friendly approach. The resort's beachfront location provides guests with easy access to the island's renowned beaches and water activities. The laid-back atmosphere ensures a relaxed stay without breaking the bank.

Trade Winds Hotel: Situated on Dickenson Bay, Trade Winds Hotel offers affordable comfort with a touch of elegance. The hotel's convenient location provides easy access to the beach, restaurants, and shopping. With spacious rooms and a welcoming ambiance, Trade Winds Hotel caters to budget-conscious travelers seeking both convenience and affordability.

These budget-friendly accommodations in Antigua cater to the practical traveler, offering a variety of options that allow visitors to experience the beauty and warmth of the island without exceeding their financial boundaries. From self-catering cottages to cozy suites, these choices ensure that exploring Antigua can be both fulfilling and economical.

Unique Stays and Local Favorites

For those with a taste for the extraordinary, Antigua opens its doors to an array of unique stays and local favorites that go beyond the traditional. These accommodations offer not only a place to rest but an opportunity to connect with the island's culture, community, and natural beauty, creating memories that extend far beyond the ordinary.

Cocobay Resort: Nestled on the western coast, Cocobay Resort is a unique, all-inclusive getaway providing guests with charming cottages overlooking the Caribbean Sea. This adults-only resort blends luxury with the natural surroundings, offering a romantic and intimate escape. With its colorful architecture and panoramic views, Cocobay Resort stands as a local favorite for couples seeking a memorable retreat.

Sugar Ridge Resort: Perched on a hillside overlooking Jolly Harbour, Sugar Ridge Resort stands as a stylish and locally celebrated option for discerning travelers. The resort's chic design, panoramic vistas, and vibrant atmosphere create a distinctive experience. Guests can indulge in spa treatments, savor local and international cuisine, and soak in the island's beauty from their private verandas.

Donkey on the Beach: Located in Ffryes Beach, Donkey on the Beach is a unique boutique hotel that captures the essence of Antigua's laid-back charm. Comprising brightly colored beach huts, this eco-friendly accommodation offers a quirky and cozy stay right on the sandy shores. Guests can wake up to the sound of the waves and bask in the simplicity of beachfront living.

Pineapple Beach Club Antigua - All-Inclusive Adults Only: Situated on Long Bay, Pineapple Beach Club Antigua is a local favorite for its all-inclusive experience and beachfront location. With a casual and relaxed atmosphere, this adults-only resort offers a taste of the island's hospitality, providing guests with an easygoing retreat filled with sun, sand, and sea.

Barbuda Cottages: For those seeking a more rustic and authentic experience, Barbuda Cottages offer a unique stay on the sister island. These charming cottages, surrounded by natural beauty, provide guests with an opportunity to immerse themselves in the tranquility of Barbuda while enjoying the warmth of local hospitality.

These unique stays and local favorites in Antigua not only offer accommodations but serve as gateways to authentic experiences. From boutique resorts to beachfront huts, each option reflects the diversity of the island's character, inviting guests to explore, connect, and create memories that resonate with the soul of Antigua.

Practical Tips for Booking Accommodations

As you embark on your journey to Antigua, securing the ideal accommodation is a crucial aspect of ensuring a seamless and enjoyable experience on the island. Here are some practical tips to guide you through the process of booking accommodations and making the most of your stay:

Book Directly for Special Deals: Consider booking directly with hotels or resorts to access special deals, promotions, or loyalty rewards. Many establishments offer exclusive perks to guests who choose to reserve directly, providing a more personalized and cost-effective experience.

Consider Seasonal Rates and Availability: Antigua experiences peak tourist seasons, influencing accommodation rates and availability. Be mindful of the timing of your visit, as rates may vary during high and low seasons. Additionally, booking well in advance ensures you secure your preferred accommodations, especially during peak travel times.

Read Reviews and Recommendations: Before finalizing your booking, read reviews and recommendations from fellow travelers on reputable platforms. Insights from those who have experienced the accommodations firsthand can offer valuable perspectives and help you make informed decisions about where to stay.

Explore Alternative Accommodations: Beyond traditional hotels, Antigua offers a range of alternative accommodations, including guesthouses, boutique hotels, and vacation rentals. Explore these options for unique and immersive experiences that align with your preferences and budget.

Flexible Dates for Cost Savings: If your travel dates are flexible, consider adjusting your itinerary to take advantage of lower rates on certain days or during specific periods. Flexibility in your travel plans can result in cost savings and a more budget-friendly stay.

Contact Accommodations Directly for Special Requests: If you have specific requests or preferences, such as room location, special occasions, or dietary needs, reach out to the accommodation directly. Many establishments are accommodating and will do their best to meet your requirements, enhancing the overall quality of your stay.

Explore Package Deals: Some travel agencies and online platforms offer package deals that include accommodations, flights, and additional perks. Explore these options to potentially find cost-effective packages that align with your travel preferences.

Check for Additional Fees and Policies: Before confirming your booking, review the accommodation's policies regarding cancellations, additional fees, and any specific requirements. Understanding these details in advance helps prevent any surprises during your stay.

Utilize Reliable Booking Platforms: When using online booking platforms, choose reputable and reliable websites to ensure the security of your reservation. Verify the authenticity of the platform, read terms and conditions, and confirm your reservation details before finalizing the booking.

Review Transportation Options: Consider the location of your chosen accommodation concerning the attractions and activities you plan to explore. Assess transportation options, proximity to public transport, and parking facilities if you intend to rent a vehicle, ensuring convenient access to the island's offerings.

By keeping these practical tips in mind, you'll be well-equipped to navigate the process of booking accommodations in Antigua, setting the stage for a memorable and enjoyable stay on this captivating Caribbean island.

CHAPTER 4: DINING AND CUISINE

Antigua's dining scene offers a rich tapestry of flavors, from gourmet restaurants to humble local eateries, each offering a unique culinary experience. For discerning palates, the island boasts a selection of the best restaurants and eateries, where chefs showcase their expertise through innovative dishes that celebrate the freshest local ingredients. These dining establishments provide a gastronomic journey, inviting diners to indulge in a symphony of flavors that reflect the diverse influences of Caribbean and international cuisine.

Delving into Antigua's culinary landscape unveils a world of local flavors and must-try dishes that capture the essence of the island's vibrant culture. From savory seafood delicacies to aromatic spices and tropical fruits, every bite tells a story of tradition and innovation. Sampling local specialties such as saltfish and fungee, pepperpot, and jerk chicken provides an opportunity to immerse oneself in the authentic flavors that define Antiguan cuisine, offering a glimpse into the heart and soul of the island's culinary heritage.

Dining in Antigua is not just about the food; it's also about the experience. With breathtaking vistas of turquoise waters and lush landscapes, dining with a view adds an extra layer of magic to every meal. Whether perched atop a cliff overlooking the Caribbean Sea or nestled among tropical gardens, restaurants and cafes offer picturesque settings that elevate the dining experience. From sunrise breakfasts to romantic sunset dinners, dining with a view in Antigua creates unforgettable moments against the backdrop of the island's natural splendor. As you embark on your culinary adventure, embracing local dining etiquette and foodie tips enhances the experience. From greeting locals with a warm "Good morning" to savoring meals with friends and family, observing these customs fosters a deeper connection with the island's culture and community. Engaging with vendors at bustling markets, exploring roadside stands for authentic street food, and embracing the laid-back island pace all contribute to a richer and more immersive dining experience in Antigua.

By embracing these local traditions and culinary insights, every meal becomes an opportunity to celebrate the vibrant flavors and warm hospitality that define Antigua's dining scene.

Best Restaurants and Eateries

Embark on a culinary journey through Antigua's best restaurants and eateries, where exquisite flavors and impeccable service converge to create unforgettable dining experiences. These establishments set the standard for excellence in gastronomy, offering a tantalizing array of culinary delights that cater to every palate and preference.

Sheer Rocks: Perched atop a rocky outcrop overlooking the azure waters of Ffryes Beach, Sheer Rocks offers a fusion of Mediterranean and Caribbean flavors. Located on the west coast of Antigua, this upscale restaurant boasts stunning sunset views and a stylish ambiance. Accessible by car, taxi, or hotel shuttle, Sheer Rocks provides an ideal setting for romantic dinners and special occasions.

Catherine's Café: Nestled in the heart of English Harbour, Catherine's Café blends French elegance with Caribbean charm. Set within the historic Nelson's Dockyard, this waterfront restaurant offers panoramic views of the harbor and marina. Guests can arrive by car or yacht, immersing themselves in the vibrant atmosphere of one of Antigua's most iconic destinations.

Le Bistro: Located in the bustling capital of St. John's, Le Bistro is a hidden gem known for its intimate atmosphere and French-inspired cuisine. Situated on Redcliffe Quay, this charming restaurant provides a tranquil escape from the city's hustle and bustle. Visitors can explore nearby shops and art galleries before enjoying a leisurely meal at this culinary oasis.

The Cove Restaurant & Bar: Tucked away on the east coast of Antigua, The Cove Restaurant & Bar offers a secluded retreat with panoramic ocean views. Accessible by car or taxi, this waterfront establishment specializes in fresh seafood and international cuisine. Guests can unwind on the restaurant's terrace, savoring the cool sea breeze and the sound of waves crashing against the shore.

Papa Zouk Fish n' Rum: A local favorite in St. John's, Papa Zouk Fish n' Rum is renowned for its laid-back atmosphere and delectable seafood dishes. Tucked away in a residential area, this cozy eatery offers an authentic Antiguan experience. Visitors can sample the catch of the day and indulge in an extensive selection of rum, soaking in the warm hospitality of this beloved establishment.

These culinary havens in Antigua promise not only exceptional cuisine but also immersive dining experiences that celebrate the island's diverse flavors and cultural heritage. Whether indulging in fine dining or savoring local delicacies, each restaurant invites guests to embark on a gastronomic adventure that lingers long after the last bite.

Local Flavors and Must-Try Dishes

In Antigua, culinary exploration unveils a rich tapestry of local flavors and must-try dishes that reflect the island's vibrant cultural heritage. From savory seafood delicacies to aromatic spices and tropical fruits, each bite tells a story of tradition and innovation, inviting visitors to immerse themselves in the authentic tastes of the Caribbean.

Saltfish and Fungee: A quintessential Antiguan dish, saltfish and fungee is a savory delight enjoyed by locals and visitors alike. Salted codfish is stewed with herbs, onions, and tomatoes, served alongside fungee, a cornmeal-based staple that complements the flavors of the fish. This hearty dish offers a taste of Antigua's culinary heritage and is a must-try for those seeking an authentic dining experience.

Pepperpot: Rich in flavor and history, pepperpot is a traditional Caribbean stew that reflects the island's diverse cultural influences. Made with a blend of meats, vegetables, and aromatic spices, including cassareep, a sauce derived from cassava, pepperpot is simmered to perfection, resulting in a dish that is both comforting and complex. Served with johnnycakes or rice, pepperpot is a favorite among locals during festive occasions and celebrations.

Jerk Chicken: Infused with fiery spices and smoky flavors, jerk chicken is a beloved dish that showcases Antigua's culinary prowess. Marinated in a blend of herbs, spices, and Scotch bonnet peppers, the chicken is grilled to perfection, resulting in tender meat with a tantalizing kick. Served with rice and peas or festival, jerk chicken is a staple of Caribbean cuisine and a must-try for visitors craving bold and zesty flavors.

Antiguan Black Pineapple: Known for its exceptional sweetness and distinctive flavor, the Antiguan black pineapple is a tropical delight that tantalizes the taste buds. Grown locally on the island, this variety of pineapple is renowned for its intense aroma and succulent texture. Whether enjoyed fresh or in refreshing cocktails and desserts, the Antiguan black pineapple offers a taste of paradise with every bite.

Coconut Bread: A beloved treat found in bakeries and roadside stalls across the island, coconut bread is a culinary gem that captures the essence of Antiguan baking. Made with grated coconut, flour, sugar, and spices, this fragrant bread is baked to golden perfection, resulting in a moist and flavorful loaf that pairs perfectly with morning coffee or afternoon tea.

From savory stews to tropical delights, Antigua's local flavors and must-try dishes offer a culinary journey that celebrates the island's rich cultural heritage and natural bounty. Whether exploring traditional eateries or sampling street food delights, each dish invites visitors to savor the vibrant flavors and warm hospitality that define Antiguan cuisine.

Dining with a View

Antigua's culinary landscape not only offers a feast for the taste buds but also presents an opportunity to dine against breathtaking backdrops, adding a visual spectacle to every meal. From clifftop panoramas to beachfront vistas, these dining establishments provide a feast for the eyes, enhancing the overall experience with a touch of natural beauty.

Cloggy's at the Antigua Yacht Club: Overlooking the historic Nelson's Dockyard, Cloggy's at the Antigua Yacht Club is a nautical-inspired dining destination. Positioned to offer expansive views of the marina and harbor, diners can enjoy their meals surrounded by the charm of sailboats and the gentle lapping of waves. The location also provides a front-row seat to witness the vibrant hues of Caribbean sunsets, transforming the dining experience into a picturesque affair.

Cecilia's High Point Café: Situated on a hill overlooking the lush landscapes of Fig Tree Drive, Cecilia's High Point Café captivates with its elevated setting. The café offers a tranquil ambiance, allowing guests to dine amidst tropical gardens while relishing panoramic views of the verdant Antiguan countryside. The elevated vantage point provides a serene escape, creating an intimate and peaceful dining retreat.

Pillars Restaurant at Admiral's Inn: Nestled within Nelson's Dockyard, Pillars Restaurant at Admiral's Inn combines historical charm with scenic views. Diners can enjoy their meals in an intimate courtyard surrounded by bougainvillea-draped walls and historic architecture. The view extends to the tranquil waters of English Harbour, making it an ideal spot to appreciate the maritime heritage of Antigua while savoring delicious cuisine.

The Lighthouse Restaurant: Perched atop a bluff on the east coast, The Lighthouse Restaurant offers a panoramic perspective of the Atlantic Ocean. Accessible by car, this clifftop dining destination provides guests with a stunning backdrop of crashing waves and endless horizons. Whether dining indoors or on the terrace, visitors can immerse themselves in the natural beauty of Antigua's coastline.

The Beach Restaurant at Curtain Bluff: Set on the southern coast, The Beach Restaurant at Curtain Bluff invites guests to dine with their toes in the sand while overlooking the Caribbean Sea. With unobstructed views of the ocean and the resort's pristine beach, this beachfront eatery provides an idyllic setting for both casual lunches and romantic dinners. The rhythmic sound of waves and gentle sea breezes add an extra layer of tranquility to the dining experience.

Dining with a view in Antigua transforms each meal into a sensory delight, where the visual splendor of the surroundings complements the exquisite flavors on the plate.

Dining Etiquette and Local Foodie Tips

In Antigua, dining etiquette reflects the island's warm hospitality and cultural traditions, ensuring that every meal is a delightful and respectful experience. Understanding local customs and embracing foodie tips enhances the enjoyment of Antigua's culinary offerings, allowing visitors to fully immerse themselves in the island's vibrant dining scene.

Greet with Warmth: Antiguans value politeness and warmth, so greeting locals with a friendly "Good morning" or "Good afternoon" sets a positive tone for interactions. Embrace the island's laid-back vibe and engage in casual conversation with restaurant staff and fellow diners, fostering a sense of camaraderie and connection.

Sample Local Specialties: To truly experience Antiguan cuisine, venture beyond familiar dishes and explore local specialties. From saltfish and fungee to pepperpot and conch fritters, sampling traditional dishes offers insight into the island's culinary heritage and diverse flavors. Be adventurous and don't hesitate to ask for recommendations from locals or restaurant staff.

Embrace Island Time: Antigua operates on its own relaxed pace, known locally as "island time." Be prepared for leisurely meals and don't rush through dining experiences. Embrace the opportunity to savor each bite, enjoy the company of loved ones, and soak in the laid-back atmosphere that defines Antiguan dining culture.

Explore Street Food: For an authentic taste of Antiguan cuisine, explore the island's vibrant street food scene. From roadside vendors selling grilled meats and seafood to colorful fruit stalls offering fresh produce, street food delights tantalize the taste buds with bold flavors and local ingredients. Embrace the opportunity to sample a variety of dishes and experience the bustling energy of local markets.

Respect Cultural Norms: When dining in Antigua, it's essential to respect cultural norms and traditions. Use utensils when provided, and avoid touching food with your hands unless it's customary to do so. Dress modestly and appropriately for dining out, especially when visiting upscale restaurants or religious establishments.

Savor Rum and Rum Punch: No visit to Antigua is complete without indulging in the island's signature libations: rum and rum punch. Sample locally produced rums and enjoy refreshing rum punch cocktails infused with tropical flavors like pineapple and coconut. Embrace the island's rum culture and raise a glass to the spirit of Antigua's culinary heritage.

Tip Graciously: Tipping is appreciated but not always expected in Antigua. If you receive exceptional service, consider leaving a gratuity of 10-15% of the bill as a token of appreciation. However, it's essential to check if a service charge has already been included in the bill before adding an additional tip.

By embracing dining etiquette and foodie tips, visitors to Antigua can elevate their culinary experiences and gain a deeper appreciation for the island's rich gastronomic heritage.

CHAPTER 5: THINGS TO DO AND OUTDOOR ACTIVITIES

Antigua beckons adventurers with a treasure trove of outdoor activities that showcase the island's natural splendor and vibrant marine life. For those eager to explore the depths of the Caribbean Sea, snorkeling and diving unveil a kaleidoscope of underwater wonders, from colorful coral reefs to schools of tropical fish. The island's crystal-clear waters provide an ideal canvas for aquatic enthusiasts to immerse themselves in an aquatic paradise, creating memories that ripple with the beauty of Antigua's marine landscapes.

As the trade winds gently sweep across Antigua's shores, sailing and yachting enthusiasts find a haven in the island's azure waters. Whether navigating the open sea or gliding into secluded coves, the maritime charm of Antigua sets the stage for an idyllic sailing experience. Yacht lovers can indulge in the island's renowned regattas, immersing themselves in a world where the sea becomes both playground and arena, echoing the maritime legacy that defines Antigua's cultural identity.

Nature enthusiasts are drawn to Antigua's lush landscapes, where hiking and nature trails offer a gateway to the island's diverse ecosystems. From the rugged paths of Fig Tree Drive to the panoramic vistas atop Signal Hill, hikers can traverse a tapestry of terrain, encountering tropical flora and fauna along the way. As the trails wind through rainforests and hilltops, the connection with Antigua's natural beauty becomes a meditative journey, offering moments of serenity and awe.

For those attuned to the melodies of birdsong, Antigua's avian wonders beckon with a symphony of chirps and calls. Bird watching enthusiasts can explore the island's habitats, from coastal wetlands to inland forests, encountering a variety of feathered residents. The colorful plumage of the Antiguan racer, the elegant frigate bird soaring over Barbuda, and the elusive West Indian whistling-duck create a harmonious chorus, inviting observers into the captivating world of Antigua's birdlife.

Antigua's beaches stand as canvases of tranquility, inviting visitors to partake in a spectrum of beach activities. From the powdery white sands of Dickenson Bay to the secluded shores of Half Moon Bay, beachgoers can bask in the sun, take refreshing dips in the turquoise waters, or engage in thrilling water sports. The beaches, framed by swaying palms and framed by azure horizons, offer a sanctuary for relaxation and adventure.

For those seeking an adrenaline rush amidst the tropical landscape, outdoor adventure tips provide essential insights. From ziplining through lush canopies to off-road expeditions across rugged terrains, adventurers can maximize their experience by understanding safety precautions and equipment usage. Antigua's outdoor adventures promise a thrilling escapade, ensuring that every leap, climb, or descent is met with both exhilaration and precaution.

In Antigua, the great outdoors become a canvas of exploration, where land and sea converge to offer a symphony of experiences. Whether delving into the depths of the Caribbean or scaling the heights of nature trails, each outdoor activity invites visitors to discover the untamed beauty that defines the heart of this Caribbean gem.

Snorkeling and Diving

Antigua's underwater realm is a mesmerizing tapestry of coral gardens and marine life, making it a haven for snorkeling and diving enthusiasts. One of the premier snorkeling spots is Cades Reef, located along the southwestern coast. Accessible by boat, this expansive coral reef system boasts vibrant coral formations and an abundance of tropical fish. Snorkelers can glide through clear waters, encountering colorful parrotfish, angel fish, and even the occasional sea turtle, creating an immersive experience that captures the essence of Antigua's marine biodiversity.

Diving enthusiasts can explore the depths of the Andes shipwreck site, a captivating underwater attraction off the coast of Deep Bay. The Andes, a 3-masted merchant ship, rests on the sandy ocean floor, offering divers an opportunity to delve into maritime history while surrounded by diverse marine life. Accessible by boat, this underwater adventure provides glimpses of reef sharks, rays, and schools of snapper, creating a dynamic and unforgettable dive experience.

Heading to the eastern coast, Green Island is a popular destination for both snorkelers and divers. With its crystal-clear waters and thriving coral formations, Green Island offers a diverse underwater landscape. Snorkelers can explore the shallow reefs, while divers can venture into deeper areas to discover underwater caves and walls teeming with marine life. The journey to Green Island typically involves a boat ride, providing an opportunity to appreciate the scenic beauty of Antigua's coastline.

For a unique diving experience, the Pillars of Hercules is a must-visit site located near the entrance to English Harbour. This underwater formation consists of towering columns of basalt rock, creating an otherworldly atmosphere. Divers can navigate through the columns, encountering marine species such as moray eels, lobsters, and reef fish. Accessible by boat, the Pillars of Hercules promise a dive that merges natural wonders with underwater exploration.

The island's commitment to marine conservation ensures that these underwater ecosystems remain pristine, inviting visitors to embark on an unforgettable journey into the depths of the Caribbean Sea.

Sailing and Yachting

Antigua, with its enchanting coastline and trade wind-kissed waters, beckons sailing and yachting enthusiasts to embark on maritime adventures. Famed for hosting some of the world's most prestigious regattas, including Antigua Sailing Week, the island is a sailing paradise that seamlessly blends the thrill of the open sea with the tranquility of secluded anchorages.

Falmouth Harbour and English Harbour stand as iconic hubs for sailing and yachting, nestled within the historic surroundings of Nelson's Dockyard. Both natural harbors offer sheltered waters, creating a haven for sailors and yachters seeking a blend of maritime history and modern amenities. The marinas provide comprehensive facilities, making them ideal starting points for nautical escapades around the island.

The annual Antigua Sailing Week, a renowned regatta attracting sailors from across the globe, transforms the seas around Antigua into a vibrant spectacle of billowing sails and competitive spirit. Participants navigate a series of races, showcasing their sailing prowess against the backdrop of the island's scenic beauty. Spectators can witness the maritime spectacle from various vantage points, immersing themselves in the electrifying atmosphere of this world-class event.

For those seeking a more leisurely sailing experience, exploring the nearby sister island of Barbuda is a captivating journey. Navigating the waters between Antigua and Barbuda allows sailors to indulge in a scenic voyage, with the possibility of encountering playful dolphins and enjoying uninterrupted views of the horizon. The pristine beaches and lagoons of Barbuda offer a serene contrast to the vibrant energy of Antigua, creating a seamless yachting escapade between two Caribbean gems.

Antigua's marinas, including Jolly Harbour and Catamaran Marina, cater to the diverse needs of sailors and yachters. These well-equipped facilities provide mooring options, essential services, and easy access to nearby attractions, ensuring a seamless and enjoyable sailing experience. From luxury yachts to sleek catamarans, Antigua invites maritime enthusiasts to navigate its turquoise waters and create lasting memories beneath the billowing sails of the Caribbean breeze.

Hiking and Nature Trails

Antigua's diverse landscapes offer a myriad of hiking and nature trails, inviting outdoor enthusiasts to explore the island's natural beauty on foot. From lush rainforests to coastal cliffs, these trails provide opportunities to immerse oneself in the island's flora, fauna, and breathtaking vistas. Lace up your hiking boots and embark on an adventure through Antigua's untamed wilderness.

Fig Tree Drive Trail: Located in the southwestern part of the island, Fig Tree Drive Trail winds through Antigua's lush rainforest, offering glimpses of towering fig trees and tropical vegetation. Accessible by car, the trailhead is marked near the village of Liberta. Hikers can trek along shaded pathways, encountering vibrant birdlife and occasional glimpses of wildlife. The trail culminates in breathtaking viewpoints overlooking the verdant landscapes of Antigua's interior.

Signal Hill Trail: Situated on the southern coast near English Harbour, Signal Hill Trail leads hikers to the island's highest point, offering panoramic views of Antigua's coastline and neighboring islands. Accessible by car or taxi, the trail begins near Shirley Heights and ascends through rugged terrain to the summit of Signal Hill. Along the way, hikers can explore historical landmarks and enjoy encounters with native flora and fauna.

Boggy Peak Trail: Formerly known as Mount Obama, Boggy Peak Trail traverses the rugged terrain of Antigua's southwestern highlands. Accessible by car, the trailhead is located near the village of Swetes. Hikers can ascend to the summit of Boggy Peak, the highest point on the island, and savor panoramic views of Antigua's coastline and interior. The trail offers a challenging yet rewarding trek through diverse ecosystems, including dry forests and rocky outcrops.

Monks Hill Trail: Nestled near English Harbour on Antigua's southern coast, Monks Hill Trail leads hikers to the ruins of Fort George, offering glimpses into the island's colonial history. Accessible by car or on foot from English Harbour, the trail winds through lush vegetation and rocky terrain, culminating in sweeping vistas of English Harbour and the surrounding coastline. History buffs and nature enthusiasts alike will find delight in this scenic hike.

Indian Town National Park Trail: Located on the northeastern coast of Antigua, Indian Town National Park Trail showcases the island's geological wonders and cultural heritage. Accessible by car, the park features hiking trails that lead to natural limestone formations, including the famous Devil's Bridge. Hikers can explore the rugged coastline, marvel at tidal blowholes, and learn about the island's indigenous Arawak heritage.

Antigua's hiking and nature trails offer a diverse range of experiences, from scenic viewpoints to cultural landmarks.

Bird Watching

Antigua, a haven for bird enthusiasts, unveils a vibrant world of feathered wonders amidst its diverse landscapes. Whether nestled within lush rainforests, coastal wetlands, or inland forests, the island's bird watching opportunities promise an auditory and visual feast for nature lovers. Grab your binoculars and embark on an avian adventure that celebrates the rich biodiversity of Antigua.

Codrington Lagoon and Frigate Bird Sanctuary: Located on the sister island of Barbuda, the Codrington Lagoon is a designated Ramsar site, and its surrounding mangroves and wetlands provide a haven for numerous bird species. Accessible by a short flight or boat ride, the sanctuary is renowned for hosting the largest colony of Magnificent Frigatebirds in the Western Hemisphere. Bird watchers can observe these majestic birds in their natural habitat, along with other coastal species, creating a mesmerizing experience.

North Sound Marine Park: Nestled on the northern coast of Antigua, the North Sound Marine Park is a haven for shorebirds and waterfowl. Accessible by boat or kayak, the park's wetlands and coastal areas attract a variety of bird species. From herons and egrets to sandpipers and plovers, bird watchers can explore the mangroves and tidal flats, capturing glimpses of both resident and migratory birds against the scenic backdrop of the North Sound.

Great Bird Island: True to its name, Great Bird Island is a paradise for bird watchers, situated just off the northeastern coast of Antigua. Accessible by boat, this protected nature reserve is home to numerous seabirds, including Brown Boobies,

Red-Billed Tropicbirds, and Magnificent Frigatebirds. Hiking trails offer opportunities to spot land birds, and the panoramic views from the island's summit enhance the overall bird watching experience.

Potworks Dam: Positioned in the interior of Antigua, Potworks Dam is a freshwater reservoir surrounded by natural vegetation. Accessible by car, this serene location is a magnet for local and migratory bird species. Bird watchers can stroll along the dam's edges, observing a variety of waterfowl, songbirds, and raptors that frequent the area. The peaceful ambiance of Potworks Dam creates a tranquil setting for bird watching enthusiasts.

Galleon Beach and Surrounding Areas: Located near English Harbour on the southern coast, Galleon Beach and its surrounding areas provide a coastal haven for bird watchers. Accessible by car, the rocky shores and coastal scrub attract a variety of seabirds, shorebirds, and migratory species. Bird watchers can explore the beach, cliffs, and nearby trails, capturing a diverse array of avian life against the backdrop of the Caribbean Sea.

Antigua's commitment to preserving its natural habitats ensures that bird watchers can enjoy a rich diversity of species in varied environments.

Beach Activities

Antigua, adorned with powdery white sands and turquoise waters, offers a haven for beachgoers seeking sun-soaked adventures and aquatic escapades. The island's diverse coastline presents a tapestry of beaches, each with its unique charm and array of activities. Whether you're a sun worshiper, water sports enthusiast, or simply seeking a tranquil shoreline retreat, Antigua's beaches invite you to indulge in the ultimate Caribbean beach experience.

Dickenson Bay: Nestled on the island's northwestern coast, Dickenson Bay is a popular stretch of pristine sands lapped by gentle waves. Accessible by car or taxi, this beach boasts a lively atmosphere with beachfront bars and water sports centers. Visitors can engage in activities like jet skiing, paddleboarding, or simply bask in the sun on rented beach chairs. The bay's calm waters make it an ideal spot for both relaxation and aquatic adventures.

Jolly Beach: Located on the west coast, Jolly Beach unfolds as a crescent of golden sands caressed by the Caribbean Sea. Accessible by car, taxi, or even a short stroll from Jolly Harbour, the beach offers a tranquil escape. Visitors can take leisurely walks along the shoreline, rent water sports equipment, or enjoy beachside dining at local restaurants. The crystal-clear waters provide an excellent setting for swimming and snorkeling.

Half Moon Bay: Tucked away on the eastern coast, Half Moon Bay is renowned for its dramatic crescent-shaped beach and powdery pink-hued sands. Accessible by car or taxi, this secluded paradise offers a serene ambiance. Beachgoers can explore the rocky outcrops, partake in beach picnics, or try body surfing in the Atlantic waves. The unspoiled beauty of Half Moon Bay makes it an ideal retreat for those seeking a tranquil beach experience.

Darkwood Beach: Situated on the southwestern coast, Darkwood Beach is framed by lush greenery and features soft sands leading into calm turquoise waters. Accessible by car or taxi, the beach exudes a relaxed vibe with swaying palm trees. Visitors can indulge in beachcombing, sunbathing, or savoring local cuisine at beachside bars. The tranquil setting and clear waters make Darkwood Beach a picturesque spot for unwinding.

Valley Church Beach: Nestled between rolling hills on the southwestern coast, Valley Church Beach enchants with its pristine sands and crystal-clear waters. Accessible by car or taxi, the beach provides a tranquil setting for relaxation and water activities. Snorkeling enthusiasts can explore the vibrant marine life near the rocky outcrops, while others can unwind with beachside massages or enjoy a casual meal at nearby restaurants.

Antigua's beaches, each offering a unique coastal experience, beckon visitors to revel in the simple joys of sun, sea, and sand.

Outdoor Adventure Tips

As you embark on outdoor adventures across Antigua's diverse landscapes, consider these tips and precautions to ensure a safe and enjoyable experience amidst the island's natural wonders.

Know the Terrain: Before venturing into the wilderness, familiarize yourself with the terrain and trail conditions. Antigua's landscapes range from rugged hills to coastal cliffs, each presenting unique challenges and hazards. Research your chosen route, including elevation changes, trail difficulty, and potential obstacles, to prepare adequately for your adventure.

Stay Hydrated: The Caribbean sun can be relentless, especially during outdoor activities. Stay hydrated by bringing an ample supply of water and electrolyte-rich beverages. Consider carrying a reusable water bottle and refill it at designated water stations or natural springs along the trails. Hydration is key to preventing heat-related illnesses and maintaining energy levels during your outdoor excursions.

Protect Yourself from the Sun: Antigua's tropical climate means abundant sunshine year-round. Protect yourself from harmful UV rays by wearing sunscreen with a high SPF rating, sunglasses with UV protection, and a wide-brimmed hat to shield your face and neck. Consider wearing lightweight, long-sleeved clothing made from breathable fabrics to minimize sun exposure while remaining comfortable during your outdoor adventures.

Bug Repellent: While exploring Antigua's natural landscapes, protect yourself from insect bites by applying insect repellent containing DEET or other effective ingredients. Mosquitoes and other biting insects may be present, especially in shaded areas and near bodies of water. Reapply repellent as needed and consider wearing light-colored clothing to minimize attracting insects.

Respect Wildlife and Habitat: Antigua is home to diverse flora and fauna, including protected species and fragile ecosystems. Respect wildlife and their habitats by observing from a distance and refraining from feeding or disturbing animals. Stay on designated trails to minimize impact on sensitive vegetation and avoid damaging delicate ecosystems.

Leave No Trace: Practice Leave No Trace principles by carrying out all trash and waste from your outdoor adventures. Pack reusable bags for collecting litter and dispose of waste responsibly in designated trash receptacles or recycling bins. Leave natural areas as you found them, preserving their beauty for future generations to enjoy.

Safety in Numbers: Consider exploring outdoor adventures with a companion or in a group, especially when venturing into remote or unfamiliar areas. Notify someone of your itinerary and expected return time, and carry a fully charged cell phone for communication in case of emergencies. Trust your instincts and avoid isolated areas, particularly at night.

By adhering to these tips and precautions, you can maximize safety and enjoyment during your outdoor adventures in Antigua. Embrace the island's natural beauty while respecting its ecosystems and wildlife, creating memorable experiences that honor the spirit of exploration and stewardship.

CHAPTER 6: ART, CULTURE AND ENTERTAINMENT

Antigua's rich cultural heritage comes to life through a tapestry of local arts, crafts, and vibrant festivals that celebrate the island's diversity. From intricately woven baskets to handcrafted pottery, local artisans showcase their talent and traditions through an array of unique creations found in markets and artisanal shops across the island. Visitors can explore the vibrant colors and intricate designs of Antiguan crafts, each piece reflecting the island's rich history and cultural influences.

Immerse yourself in Antigua's cultural narrative by visiting museums and galleries that showcase the island's artistic legacy. From the Museum of Antigua and Barbuda to contemporary art galleries, these cultural institutions offer insights into the island's history, heritage, and artistic expressions. Visitors can admire works by local and international artists, delve into Antigua's colonial past, and gain a deeper appreciation for the island's diverse cultural tapestry.

Antigua's calendar is brimming with lively festivals and events that celebrate music, dance, and local traditions. From the pulsating rhythms of Carnival to the vibrant colors of the Antigua Sailing Week Regatta, these annual celebrations offer a glimpse into the island's spirited culture and community. Visitors can immerse themselves in the infectious energy of street parades, live performances, and cultural showcases, creating unforgettable memories steeped in the vibrancy of Antiguan life.

As the sun sets, Antigua's nightlife scene comes alive with an array of entertainment options, from beachfront bars to vibrant nightclubs. Whether you're sipping cocktails at a sunset lounge or dancing to the rhythm of Caribbean beats, the island offers something for every taste and mood. Local musicians and DJs set the stage for unforgettable evenings filled with laughter, music, and camaraderie, providing a quintessential Caribbean nightlife experience.

For those seeking unique souvenirs and treasures to commemorate their Antiguan adventure, the island's local markets and shops offer a treasure trove of handmade crafts, artwork, and authentic souvenirs. From bustling street markets to quaint boutiques, visitors can peruse a diverse selection of locally-made goods, including handmade jewelry, woven textiles, and artisanal spices. Shopping in Antigua is not just about acquiring keepsakes; it's about connecting with the island's culture and supporting local artisans and businesses.

Local Arts and Crafts

Venture into the heart of Antigua's cultural tapestry by exploring the vibrant realm of local arts and crafts. The island's artisans, deeply rooted in tradition, showcase their talents through a diverse array of handcrafted treasures. One such hub is the quaint village of Falmouth, where the Antigua and Barbuda Craft Market comes to life. Nestled near the historic Nelson's Dockyard, this market is a haven for those seeking authentic Antiguan craftsmanship.

As you stroll through the market, you'll encounter skilled artisans crafting intricate items such as handmade pottery, woven baskets, and vibrant textiles. Engage in conversations with the local craftspeople, gaining insights into their techniques and the stories behind each creation. The Craft Market is not just a shopping destination; it's a cultural experience where the essence of Antiguan heritage unfolds through the hands of its talented artisans.

Another hotspot for discovering local arts and crafts is the Redcliffe Quay in the capital city of St. John's. This historic area, adorned with colorful colonial-style buildings, houses a variety of boutique shops and galleries. Here, you can peruse a curated collection of locally-made artworks, jewelry, and crafts. The ambiance of Redcliffe Quay, coupled with the authenticity of the handmade items, creates a delightful shopping experience for those seeking unique and meaningful souvenirs.

For a truly immersive encounter with Antigua's artistic community, make your way to Fig Tree Studio Art Gallery in English Harbour. This intimate gallery space showcases the works of both local and international artists, providing a platform for creative expression. The gallery's eclectic collection includes paintings, sculptures, and mixed-media pieces, reflecting the dynamic spirit of Antigua's art scene. Visiting Fig Tree Studio is not just about observing art; it's an opportunity to connect with the island's cultural pulse and perhaps take home a piece of Antiguan creativity.

Whether exploring the vibrant Craft Market in Falmouth, discovering treasures at Redcliffe Quay, or delving into the artistic realm of Fig Tree Studio, Antigua's local arts and crafts scene invites you to embrace the island's cultural heritage through the lens of its talented artisans. Each creation tells a story, and every piece carries the essence of Antigua's rich and diverse artistic traditions.

Museums and Galleries

Embarking on a cultural odyssey in Antigua involves delving into the captivating realm of museums and galleries that beautifully preserve the island's heritage. These cultural repositories offer a window into the past, showcasing the art, history, and narratives that shape Antigua's identity.

Museum of Antigua and Barbuda: Located in the capital city of St. John's, the Museum of Antigua and Barbuda stands as a cultural cornerstone. Housed in the historic Colonial Court House, this museum chronicles the island's history from its indigenous roots to the present day. Exhibits include artifacts, documents, and multimedia displays, providing a comprehensive understanding of Antigua's diverse heritage. The museum's central location in St. John's makes it easily accessible for those keen on unraveling the layers of Antiguan history.

Fig Tree Studio Art Gallery: Situated in the scenic English Harbour, Fig Tree Studio Art Gallery transcends the conventional gallery experience. This intimate space celebrates the fusion of local and international artistic expressions. Visitors can explore a curated collection of paintings, sculptures, and mixed-media artworks that capture the essence of Antigua's creative spirit. The gallery's location near Nelson's Dockyard makes it a captivating stop for art enthusiasts seeking a blend of culture and maritime history.

National Sailing Academy Gallery: Nestled within the premises of the National Sailing Academy in English Harbour, this gallery merges the worlds of art and maritime activities. Showcasing the works of local artists, the gallery offers a unique perspective on Antigua's connection to the sea. Visitors can admire maritime-themed artworks while appreciating the picturesque views of sailboats against the backdrop of English Harbour. The gallery's strategic location makes it a seamless addition to a day of exploring the historic naval attractions in the area.

Heritage Quay Museum: Situated in the heart of St. John's, Heritage Quay Museum provides a curated journey through Antigua's cultural and historical narrative. The museum, housed in a modern facility, features exhibits that span the island's indigenous heritage, colonial history, and post-independence developments. Visitors can explore galleries dedicated to archaeology, slavery, and the island's vibrant Carnival traditions. Conveniently located in the bustling capital, Heritage Quay Museum offers a cultural retreat for those eager to delve into Antigua's multifaceted past.

Island Art Gallery and Cafe: Tucked away in the serene surroundings of Runaway Bay, the Island Art Gallery and Cafe offers a tranquil haven for art lovers. This gallery, adorned with Caribbean-inspired artworks, allows visitors to immerse themselves in the local art scene while enjoying the laid-back ambiance. The onsite cafe adds a delightful culinary dimension to the experience, inviting guests to savor refreshments amidst the artistic charm. The gallery's location near the beach provides a perfect blend of art, relaxation, and scenic beauty.

Each museum and gallery in Antigua is a testament to the island's commitment to preserving and showcasing its cultural legacy.

Festivals and Events

Antigua comes alive with a vibrant tapestry of festivals and events throughout the year, each weaving a unique story of the island's rich cultural heritage and lively spirit.

Antigua Carnival: A pinnacle of festivity, Antigua Carnival stands as one of the Caribbean's most dynamic celebrations. Held annually in late July to early August, this extravaganza features colorful street parades, lively music, and elaborate costumes. Locals and visitors alike revel in the infectious energy, dancing to the rhythms of calypso and soca music. The carnival's Grand Parade, J'ouvert morning festivities, and vibrant T-shirt bands contribute to an unforgettable cultural experience.

Antigua Sailing Week Regatta: For enthusiasts of maritime adventures, the Antigua Sailing Week Regatta, typically held in late April to early May, is a highlight on the island's calendar. This world-renowned sailing event attracts yachts and sailors from around the globe to compete in exhilarating races along Antigua's pristine coastline. Spectators can witness the spectacular sight of billowing sails against the Caribbean Sea while enjoying shoreside parties and social events.

Independence Day Celebrations: Antigua and Barbuda gained independence from the United Kingdom on November 1st, 1981, and the nation commemorates this significant milestone with grand Independence Day celebrations. Festivities include cultural performances, parades, and patriotic displays, fostering a sense of national pride and unity. Locals and visitors alike join in the festivities, showcasing the spirit of independence that defines the nation.

Wadadli Day Festival: Wadadli Day, celebrated on November 1st, is a cultural festival that honors the island's heritage and artistic achievements. The day pays homage to the indigenous Arawak people, the original inhabitants of Antigua. Festivities include cultural exhibitions, traditional performances, and artistic showcases, allowing attendees to immerse themselves in the island's rich cultural tapestry.

South Coast Horizons Eco Adventure Festival: For those passionate about environmental conservation and outdoor activities, the South Coast Horizons Eco Adventure Festival is a must-attend event. Held annually, this festival promotes eco-friendly practices and showcases the natural beauty of Antigua's south coast. Activities include guided nature walks, bird watching, and educational programs focused on sustainability and environmental awareness.

Antigua's festivals and events offer a kaleidoscope of experiences, inviting visitors to participate in the island's cultural vibrancy and celebratory spirit.

Nightlife and Entertainment

As the sun dips below the horizon, Antigua transforms into a lively canvas of nightlife and entertainment, offering an array of experiences to suit every taste.

English Harbour's Dockside Diversions: The historic English Harbour stands as a hub for nocturnal adventures. Enjoy the laid-back atmosphere at bars like Catherine's Café Plage, where beachside elegance meets live music, creating a perfect setting for a relaxed evening. Venture to Abracadabra Restaurant & Disco-Bar, an iconic establishment where the transition from dining to dancing seamlessly harmonizes with the beats of the night. The allure of English Harbour's nightlife lies not only in its diverse establishments but also in the backdrop of historic Nelson's Dockyard, which adds a touch of maritime charm to the experience.

St. John's Nighttime Delights: The capital city, St. John's, pulsates with energy as night falls. Start your evening at Quin Farara's Irish Pub, a lively spot where live music and a welcoming atmosphere set the tone for a memorable night. For those seeking a bit of sophistication, the rooftop lounge at The Blockhouse offers panoramic views of St. John's and a curated selection of cocktails. Explore the streets of St. John's to discover hidden gems like C & C Wine House, where the intimate ambiance and live music create a cozy retreat.

Beachfront Bliss at Darkwood Beach: Darkwood Beach isn't just for daytime sunbathing; it also sets the stage for enchanting beachfront evenings. The Darkwood Beach Bar transforms as the sun sets, becoming a beach party haven with live music, cocktails, and a bonfire. The rhythmic sounds of the Caribbean blend with the gentle lapping of waves, creating a magical ambiance that encapsulates the essence of Antigua's tropical nights.

Shirley Heights Lookout: For an elevated nightlife experience, venture to Shirley Heights Lookout. Every Sunday, the hilltop comes alive with the sounds of steel pan music and reggae beats during the renowned Shirley Heights Sunset Party. Revel in the panoramic views of English Harbour and Falmouth Harbour while dancing to the infectious rhythms. The weekly gathering attracts both locals and visitors, creating a spirited atmosphere that encapsulates the island's social heartbeat.

Falmouth's Waterside Charms: Falmouth Harbour offers a blend of waterfront charm and lively entertainment. Explore the ambiance at Cloggy's Café, a waterside venue where yachts dock, and live music permeates the air. The combination of maritime vistas and rhythmic tunes creates an unparalleled evening experience. Nearby, South Point Antigua offers a stylish rooftop lounge, providing a sophisticated setting for sipping cocktails and enjoying the island's nighttime panorama.

Antigua's nightlife is a dynamic fusion of Caribbean rhythms, coastal charm, and vibrant gatherings. Whether you're dancing under the stars at Shirley Heights or savoring beachfront bliss at Darkwood, the island's evenings promise an unforgettable tapestry of experiences for every nocturnal adventurer.

Local Markets, Shopping, and Souvenirs

Exploring Antigua's local markets and shopping districts is not just about acquiring treasures; it's a journey into the heart of the island's vibrant culture and craftsmanship.

St. John's Market Street: Begin your shopping escapade in the bustling heart of St. John's, where Market Street comes alive with an array of shops and vendors. Meander through the vibrant stalls of the Public Market, where locals showcase fresh produce, spices, and handmade crafts. Engage with friendly vendors, sample exotic fruits, and immerse yourself in the colorful atmosphere. The adjacent streets house boutiques and souvenir shops, such as Heritage Quay and Redcliffe Quay, offering an eclectic mix of local crafts, clothing, and Caribbean-inspired keepsakes.

Antigua and Barbuda Craft Market in Falmouth: Head to the charming village of Falmouth, where the Antigua and Barbuda Craft Market beckons with a kaleidoscope of handmade treasures. Nestled near the historic Nelson's Dockyard, this market is a haven for those seeking authentic Antiguan craftsmanship. Explore stalls adorned with locally-made jewelry, pottery, and textiles, each item narrating a story of the island's artistic heritage. The Craft Market is not just a shopping destination; it's an immersion into Antigua's cultural tapestry.

English Harbour's Artisanal Boutiques: Delve into the artisanal boutiques surrounding English Harbour, where unique finds await. Explore establishments like Colibri Boutiques, offering an exquisite collection of Caribbean-inspired jewelry and accessories. The intimate setting and personalized service make for a delightful shopping experience. Nearby, ZEMI Art Gallery showcases the works of local artists, providing an opportunity to bring home a piece of Antigua's artistic spirit.

Duty-Free Delights at Heritage Quay: If you're in search of duty-free deals and a diverse shopping experience, look no further than Heritage Quay in St. John's. This shopping complex houses a variety of stores, from international brands to local boutiques. Explore a curated selection of jewelry, fashion, and electronics, all within a vibrant and duty-free setting. The lively atmosphere and diverse offerings make Heritage Quay a one-stop destination for retail therapy.

Runaway Bay's Seaside Shopping: For a shopping experience with a backdrop of turquoise waters, head to Runaway Bay. Explore the retail offerings at Epicurean Fine Foods and Pharmacy, where you can find gourmet delights, local products, and a variety of souvenirs. The convenience of combining grocery shopping with souvenir hunting makes this spot a unique destination for travelers.

Antigua's markets and shopping venues are not merely places to shop; they are cultural hubs where the island's creativity and commerce converge.

CHAPTER 7: 7-DAY ITINERARY IN ANTIGUA AND BARBUDA

Day 1: Arrival and Introduction to Antigua

Morning: Upon arrival at V.C. Bird International Airport, you'll be greeted by the warm Caribbean breeze and the inviting atmosphere of Antigua. After clearing customs and immigration, make your way to your accommodation to settle in and freshen up for the day ahead. Whether you're staying in one of the luxurious resorts along Dickenson Bay or opting for a charming guesthouse in English Harbour, take a moment to appreciate the island's hospitality and breathtaking vistas.

Afternoon: After a rejuvenating start to your day, venture out to explore the historic heart of St. John's, the capital city of Antigua. Begin your journey at Heritage Quay, where duty-free shopping and waterfront views beckon. Dive into the vibrant streets lined with colorful colonial buildings, and make your way to the Museum of Antigua and Barbuda to delve into the island's rich history and culture. For lunch, indulge in local flavors at one of the charming cafes or waterfront restaurants, savoring dishes like pepperpot and fungi.

Evening: As the sun begins to set, head to Shirley Heights Lookout for a quintessential Antiguan experience. Join locals and fellow travelers at the famed Shirley Heights Sunset Party, where panoramic views of English Harbour provide the backdrop for live music and dancing. Savor delicious barbecue fare and sip on rum punch as you soak in the lively atmosphere. Toast to the beginning of your Antiguan adventure and anticipate the unforgettable experiences that lie ahead.

Day 2: Island Exploration and Beach Bliss

Morning: Rise with the sun and embark on an island adventure to discover the natural wonders of Antigua. Start your day with a visit to Devil's Bridge, a captivating natural limestone arch carved by the relentless force of the Atlantic Ocean. Take in the breathtaking coastal views and feel the spray of the crashing waves against the rugged cliffs. Don't forget your camera to capture the beauty of this iconic landmark.

Afternoon: After exploring Devil's Bridge, make your way to Half Moon Bay, renowned for its pristine white sands and crystal-clear waters. Spend the afternoon basking in the Caribbean sunshine, swimming in the turquoise sea, or simply relaxing under the shade of a palm tree. The beach's tranquil ambiance and untouched beauty make it a perfect retreat for unwinding and rejuvenating.

Evening: As evening approaches, indulge in a culinary journey at one of Antigua's seaside restaurants. Dine al fresco at one of the beachfront eateries along Dickenson Bay or Ffryes Beach, where you can savor freshly caught seafood and Caribbean-inspired delicacies. Let the soothing sound of the waves serenade you as you indulge in a memorable dining experience overlooking the ocean.

Day 3: Adventure in the Rainforest and Secluded Bliss

Morning: Embark on an exhilarating adventure in Antigua's lush rainforest with a visit to the Antigua Rainforest Canopy Tour. Glide through the treetops on zip lines, taking in panoramic views of the verdant landscape. The tour combines adventure with eco-awareness, providing a unique perspective on the island's diverse flora and fauna.

Afternoon: After an adrenaline-filled morning, seek tranquility at Darkwood Beach. This secluded gem is framed by swaying palms and offers powdery sand that invites you to unwind. Snorkel in the clear waters, explore the marine life, or simply savor the serenity. Pack a picnic or indulge in local cuisine at a beachside café for a leisurely afternoon.

Evening: Head back to your accommodation to refresh, then venture out to explore Falmouth Harbor. Dine at one of the harborfront restaurants, where you can enjoy freshly prepared seafood while watching the yachts gently bobbing in the harbor. After dinner, take a stroll along the marina, absorbing the vibrant atmosphere of this maritime haven.

Day 4: Historical Encounters and Beach Bliss

Morning: Begin your day with a visit to Nelson's Dockyard, a UNESCO World Heritage Site and the only continuously working Georgian naval dockyard in the world. Explore the historic structures, museums, and maritime exhibits that offer a glimpse into Antigua's naval history. Take a guided tour to fully appreciate the significance of this colonial marvel.

Afternoon: For an afternoon of beach bliss, head to Fort James Beach. This picturesque stretch of sand is overlooked by the ruins of Fort James, providing a unique blend of history and relaxation. Swim in the azure waters, soak up the sun, and explore the historic fort for panoramic views of St. John's Harbor.

Evening: Conclude your day with a delightful dinner in the heart of St. John's. Explore the local eateries and street vendors offering a variety of culinary delights. Whether you opt for a casual Caribbean meal or fine dining, let the evening unfold with the flavors of Antiguan cuisine.

Day 5: Barbuda's Frigate Bird Sanctuary Excursion

Morning: Embark on a day trip to Barbuda, just a short ferry or plane ride away. Begin your Barbuda adventure with a visit to the Frigate Bird Sanctuary, home to one of the largest colonies of magnificent frigatebirds in the world. Witness the incredible spectacle of these graceful birds soaring overhead and nesting in the mangroves.

Afternoon: After the bird sanctuary, relax on the pink sand beaches of Barbuda, such as Princess Diana Beach or Coco Point. Enjoy a leisurely beach day, swimming in the crystalline waters or strolling along the pristine shoreline. Barbuda's unspoiled beauty offers a serene escape from the hustle and bustle.

Evening: Return to Antigua in the evening and unwind with a delicious dinner at a beachfront restaurant in Dickenson Bay. Reflect on the day's adventures while enjoying a seafood feast or Caribbean-inspired dishes.

Day 6: Outdoor Exploration and Sunset Serenity

Morning: Venture to Great Bird Island, a nature lover's paradise located just off the coast of Antigua. This tiny uninhabited island is a sanctuary for seabirds, and its coral reefs offer excellent snorkeling opportunities. Explore the walking trails, encounter indigenous wildlife, and enjoy the serene surroundings.

Afternoon: After your island exploration, head to the charming village of Falmouth for a late lunch at one of the local cafes. Experience the laid-back atmosphere and savor delicious Caribbean cuisine while taking in views of the harbor.

Evening: Conclude your penultimate day in Antigua with a sunset cruise. Sail along the coastline, enjoying the changing hues of the sky as the sun dips below the horizon. Many operators offer evening cruises with dinner on board, providing a magical experience as the stars emerge.

Day 7: Leisurely Farewell and Departure

Morning: On your final day, take it slow and savor your last moments in Antigua. Enjoy a leisurely breakfast at a beachfront café or at your accommodation. If you have any last-minute shopping or souvenirs to pick up, explore the local markets or boutiques.

Afternoon: Spend your final afternoon at one of Antigua's stunning beaches, perhaps revisiting a favorite spot or discovering a new one. Relax, swim, and soak up the sun, creating lasting memories of your time in the Caribbean.

Evening: As the day winds down, reflect on your Antiguan adventure over a farewell dinner. Choose a restaurant with a romantic ambiance or a lively spot with live music to celebrate your journey. Relish in the flavors, the culture, and the beauty of Antigua one last time before bidding the island farewell.

CHAPTER 8: PRACTICAL INFORMATION AND TIPS

Etiquette and Customs

In Antigua, embracing local customs and displaying respect for cultural etiquette enhances your overall experience and fosters meaningful interactions with the island's residents. Here are some insights into Antiguan etiquette and customs to help you navigate the social landscape:

Respect for Locals: Antiguans take pride in their culture and traditions. Show respect for local customs, such as greeting others with a warm smile and a friendly "Good morning" or "Good afternoon." Demonstrating genuine interest in the island's heritage and engaging respectfully with locals fosters positive connections.

Dress Code: While Antigua boasts a laid-back atmosphere, modest attire is appreciated when visiting public places, religious sites, or dining establishments. Beachwear is suitable for the beach, but cover-ups are advisable when venturing into town or dining at restaurants.

Greetings and Gestures: Handshakes are a common form of greeting in Antigua, particularly in formal settings. When meeting someone for the first time, a firm handshake accompanied by eye contact is customary. Additionally, it's courteous to address individuals with their titles, such as "Mr." or "Ms.," followed by their last name until invited to use their first name.

Social Courtesy: Politeness and courtesy are highly valued in Antiguan culture. Remember to use "please" and "thank you" in your interactions, whether you're ordering a meal, requesting assistance, or engaging in conversation. Being gracious and appreciative of hospitality goes a long way in fostering positive relationships.

Respect for Elders: In Antiguan society, respect for elders is deeply ingrained. When interacting with older individuals, demonstrate deference and attentiveness. It's customary to greet elders with a friendly nod or a respectful greeting, acknowledging their wisdom and experience.

Religious Observances: Antigua is home to diverse religious communities, and religious observances are an integral part of the island's cultural tapestry. Show respect for religious sites and customs, such as removing hats and maintaining a quiet demeanor when visiting churches or places of worship.

Environmental Consciousness: Antiguans hold a deep reverence for their natural surroundings. Help preserve the island's pristine environment by practicing eco-friendly behaviors, such as avoiding littering, conserving water and energy, and supporting sustainable tourism initiatives.

By embracing Antigua's etiquette and customs with openness and respect, you'll forge meaningful connections with the island's residents and gain deeper insights into its rich cultural heritage. Your mindful approach to social interactions will enrich your travel experience and leave a positive impression on those you encounter during your journey.

Language and Communication

Antigua and Barbuda, with its vibrant cultural mosaic, showcases a unique linguistic tapestry that reflects the island's rich history and diverse heritage. Here's a glimpse into the language and communication nuances that will enhance your interactions during your stay:

Official Language: English serves as the official language of Antigua and Barbuda, making communication accessible for international visitors. The local Antiguan Creole, often referred to as "Antiguan Dialect" or "Patois," also adds a flavorful touch to daily conversations. While English is widely spoken, you might encounter Antiguans using elements of the local Creole, which adds a distinctive rhythm to the spoken word.

Greetings and Expressions: Antiguans are known for their warm and friendly demeanor, and greetings play a significant role in daily interactions. Common greetings include "Good morning," "Good afternoon," and "Good evening." Embrace the laid-back atmosphere by using these pleasantries when engaging with locals, and don't be surprised if you receive a warm smile in return.

Patois Expressions: While English is the primary language, you may encounter Antiguans using Patois expressions, especially in casual settings. Phrases like "Wha gwan?" (What's going on?) or "Mi deh yah" (I am here) add a local flair to conversations. Feel free to immerse yourself in the island's linguistic charm and ask for explanations if you're curious about specific expressions.

Non-Verbal Communication: Non-verbal communication is an essential aspect of Antiguan interaction. Maintain eye contact during conversations as a sign of attentiveness and respect. Additionally, non-verbal gestures, such as a nod or a friendly wave, are common ways to convey understanding or greeting, adding a layer of warmth to exchanges.

Tone and Rhythm: The rhythmic quality of Antiguan speech is reflective of the island's vibrant culture. Antiguans often infuse a melodic tone into their conversations, creating an engaging and expressive mode of communication. Embrace the musicality of the local language, and you'll find that the island's linguistic cadence contributes to the overall charm of your experience.

Cultural Sensitivity: As in any destination, cultural sensitivity is key to effective communication. Listen actively, be open to different expressions, and approach conversations with a genuine interest in the island's cultural diversity. Demonstrating respect for local customs and linguistic nuances fosters positive connections and enriches your overall experience.

Embracing the language and communication styles of Antigua and Barbuda allows you to connect more authentically with the island's residents. Whether engaging in English or savoring the local Patois expressions, your willingness to embrace the linguistic charm enhances the cultural journey during your stay.

Health and Safety Tips

As you embark on your Antiguan adventure, prioritizing your health and safety ensures a seamless and enjoyable experience on this sun-soaked paradise. Here are essential tips to safeguard your well-being while immersing yourself in the natural beauty of Antigua and Barbuda:

Sun Protection: The Caribbean sun is blissfully warm, but it's crucial to shield yourself from its intensity. Pack and regularly apply high SPF sunscreen, wear a wide-brimmed hat, and don stylish sunglasses to protect your skin and eyes from the sun's rays. Hydrate consistently to stay refreshed in the tropical climate.

Hydration and Nutrition: Antigua's warm climate emphasizes the importance of staying hydrated. Carry a reusable water bottle and drink plenty of fluids throughout the day, especially if engaging in outdoor activities. Explore the local cuisine, rich in fresh fruits and seafood, for a delightful and nourishing culinary experience.

Mosquito Precautions: While Antigua is generally mosquito-friendly, it's advisable to take precautions. Apply insect repellent, particularly during dawn and dusk when mosquitoes are most active. Consider wearing long sleeves and pants in the evenings, especially if venturing into areas with dense vegetation.

Safe Swimming Practices: Antigua boasts stunning beaches with inviting waters, but it's essential to practice safe swimming. Pay attention to water conditions, especially if venturing to more remote areas. Swim in designated areas with lifeguards, and be mindful of strong currents, particularly on the Atlantic side of the island.

Medical Precautions: Antigua offers quality medical services, but it's wise to carry a basic first aid kit with essentials like bandages, pain relievers, and any personal medications you may need. Familiarize yourself with the location of medical facilities, and keep emergency numbers on hand.

Responsible Exploration: Whether hiking nature trails or exploring historical sites, responsible exploration is key to safety. Wear appropriate footwear, follow designated paths, and adhere to any safety guidelines provided at attractions. If engaging in outdoor activities, consider informing someone about your plans and expected return time.

Local Wildlife Awareness: Antigua is home to diverse flora and fauna. Exercise caution around wildlife, and avoid touching or feeding animals. If venturing into natural areas, be aware of your surroundings and respect the natural habitats of the island's indigenous species.

Safe Transportation Practices: If renting a vehicle or using local transportation, prioritize safety. Follow traffic rules, wear seatbelts, and exercise caution, especially on winding roads. If relying on public transportation, be aware of schedules and plan accordingly.

Emergency Preparedness: Familiarize yourself with the location of your country's embassy or consulate in Antigua. Keep important documents, including identification and travel insurance details, secure and easily accessible. In case of an emergency, contact local authorities or seek assistance from your embassy.

By incorporating these health and safety tips into your Antiguan journey, you not only safeguard your well-being but also enhance your ability to fully immerse yourself in the island's captivating experiences. Embrace the spirit of responsible travel, and you'll create lasting memories in this Caribbean haven.

Emergency Contacts

During your stay in Antigua and Barbuda, having access to emergency contacts ensures swift assistance and peace of mind in unexpected situations. Here are vital numbers and resources to keep handy throughout your journey:

Police Emergency:
Dial 911 for immediate police assistance in case of emergencies, criminal incidents, or accidents requiring law enforcement intervention.

Medical Emergencies:
For medical emergencies, dial 911 or visit the nearest hospital or medical facility for urgent medical attention.
Mount St. John's Medical Centre: +1 (268) 484-2700
Holberton Hospital: +1 (268) 462-0251

Fire and Rescue Services:
In the event of fires, accidents, or other emergencies requiring fire and rescue services, dial 911 for immediate assistance.

Coast Guard and Marine Emergencies:
Antigua Coast Guard: +1 (268) 462-0368
In marine emergencies or distress at sea, contact the Antigua Coast Guard for assistance and rescue operations.

Embassy and Consulate Information:
United States Embassy in Antigua and Barbuda: +1 (268) 463-6531
British High Commission in Antigua and Barbuda: +1 (268) 462-0008

Canadian High Commission in Barbados (responsible for Antigua and Barbuda): +1 (246) 629-3550

Local Tourist Information:
Antigua and Barbuda Tourism Authority: +1 (268) 562-7600
For inquiries about tourist attractions, accommodations, and general travel information, contact the Antigua and Barbuda.

Tourism Authority.Non-Emergency Police Assistance:
For non-emergency police assistance, contact the Antigua and Barbuda Police Force at their general inquiries line: +1 (268) 462-0125.

Prioritize your safety and well-being by familiarizing yourself with these essential emergency contacts. Whether you require medical assistance, police intervention, or consular services, knowing where to turn in times of need ensures a seamless and secure travel experience in Antigua and Barbuda.

Communication and Internet Access

Ensuring seamless communication and staying connected during your Antiguan getaway enhances your travel experience. Here's a guide to navigating communication and internet access on the vibrant islands of Antigua and Barbuda:

Mobile Networks:
Antigua and Barbuda feature well-established mobile networks, offering reliable coverage across the islands. Major carriers include Digicel and Flow. Ensure your mobile device is unlocked before arrival to use local SIM cards for cost-effective plans and local numbers.

Internet Access:
Most accommodations, including hotels, resorts, and guesthouses, provide Wi-Fi access. Confirm the availability and details of internet services with your chosen accommodation upon arrival.

Public Wi-Fi:
Public places such as cafes, restaurants, and some tourist attractions offer free Wi-Fi access. While exploring, take advantage of these hotspots to stay connected without using your mobile data.

Internet Cafés:
Antigua and Barbuda have internet cafés in major towns, offering computer access and internet services for a nominal fee. This option is useful if you don't have a personal device or need extended access.

Mobile Data Plans:
Local carriers offer various prepaid data plans for tourists. Purchase a data plan that aligns with your internet usage needs, allowing you to access maps, stay in touch with loved ones, and share your Antiguan experiences on social media.

Communication Apps:
Utilize communication apps such as WhatsApp, Skype, and FaceTime for cost-effective ways to stay in touch with friends and family internationally. These apps work well over Wi-Fi and mobile data networks.

Postal Services:
While traditional postal services are available, the use of email and other digital communication methods is more efficient. If sending postcards or packages, inquire about local postal services at your accommodation or local post offices.
Stay connected effortlessly in Antigua and Barbuda by leveraging local mobile networks, Wi-Fi hotspots, and communication apps.

Embracing these communication options ensures you can stay in touch with loved ones and make the most of your Caribbean escape.

Useful Apps, Websites, and Maps

Embarking on an adventure in Antigua and Barbuda becomes even more enjoyable with the aid of useful apps, websites, and maps that cater to travelers. Here are some recommendations to enhance your experience on the islands:

Antigua and Barbuda Tourism Guide (www.antiguabarbuda.com): The official tourism app provides comprehensive information on attractions, events, and local services. Navigate the islands with ease and discover hidden gems along the way.

Maps.Me (www.maps.me): Download offline maps of Antigua and Barbuda through Maps.Me for easy navigation without the need for a constant internet connection. Explore the islands, locate attractions, and plan your routes effortlessly.

TripAdvisor (www.tripadvisor.com): Gain insights into the best dining spots, attractions, and accommodations in Antigua and Barbuda through traveler reviews on TripAdvisor. Access valuable recommendations and firsthand experiences shared by fellow adventurers.

Antigua and Barbuda Tourism Authority (www.visitantiguabarbuda.com): Explore the official tourism website for up-to-date information on events, accommodations, and must-visit destinations. The site offers valuable insights to plan your itinerary effectively.

Antigua Nice (www.antiguanice.com): Antigua Nice is a local online guide offering information on events, dining, activities, and services. Stay informed about current happenings and local offerings through this comprehensive resource.

Waze (www.waze.com): Waze is a reliable navigation app that provides real-time traffic updates, road conditions, and optimal routes. Use Waze to navigate Antigua's roads efficiently and reach your destinations with ease.
Weather Updates:

Weather.com (www.weather.com): Stay informed about the local weather forecast through Weather.com. Access current conditions, extended forecasts, and essential weather information to plan your activities accordingly.
Currency Conversion:

XE Currency Converter (www.xe.com): For quick and accurate currency conversions, use the XE Currency Converter app or website. Stay informed about exchange rates and manage your budget effectively during your stay.
Emergency Services:

911Caribbean Emergency Services (www.911caribbean.com): This website provides emergency contact information for Antigua and Barbuda, including police, medical, and fire services. Keep this resource handy for quick access to essential services.

Leverage these apps, websites, and maps to enhance your travel experience in Antigua and Barbuda. Whether you're exploring the historical wonders of Nelson's Dockyard or seeking the perfect beachside retreat, these tools ensure you make the most of your Caribbean journey.

CONCLUSION

As we draw the final curtain on this journey through the sun-kissed landscapes of Antigua and Barbuda, I hope the pages of this guide have unfolded the vibrant tapestry of experiences that await you. From the historic cobblestones of Nelson's Dockyard to the tranquil shores of Darkwood Beach, these islands have whispered tales of resilience, celebrated nature's bounty, and painted unforgettable memories.

Antigua and Barbuda, with their azure waters and golden shores, invite you to witness a living masterpiece. The colonial echoes at Shirley Heights, the rhythmic rustle of palm trees at Falmouth Harbor, and the awe-inspiring spectacle of Devil's Bridge weave a narrative that goes beyond the pages of any guidebook. It's a tale of a nation proud of its heritage and eager to share its treasures.

From savoring the zest of local flavors at Betty's Hope to dining with a view at Shirley Heights, every bite in Antigua is a celebration of its rich cultural tapestry. The warmth of the locals, their penchant for storytelling, and the rhythm of local festivals create a melody that resonates through the cobblestone streets of St. John's.

For the seekers of outdoor thrills, Antigua and Barbuda are playgrounds of possibility. Dive into the crystal-clear waters for a snorkeling escapade, set sail on the Caribbean breeze, or find solace in the embrace of nature along the hiking trails. The islands beckon you to explore, to discover, and to be rejuvenated by the natural wonders that surround you.

The rich tapestry of Antiguan culture is woven with threads of history, music, and vibrant celebrations. The lively beats of local festivals, the artistic expressions in museums and galleries, and the melody of Patois expressions create an atmosphere where you'll find yourself dancing to the rhythm of the islands.

As you put down this guide, I invite you to carry the essence of Antigua and Barbuda in your heart. Prepare to be embraced by the warmth of the Caribbean sun, to lose yourself in the vibrant hues of the coral reefs, and to become part of a narrative that transcends time. The islands await your footsteps, and the stories you'll create here will become cherished chapters in your own travelogue.

Get ready to be captivated, get ready to be enchanted, get ready to visit Antigua and Barbuda—a treasure trove of beauty, culture, and adventure that promises an experience beyond imagination.

Made in the USA
Columbia, SC
25 September 2024

43002748R00072